❧

Jack Oakley was born in Dudley, Worcestershire in 1931, though reared in Upper Gornal, a Black Country village whose inhabitants spoke a dialect even other West Midlanders found almost incomprehensible. Added to this linguistic confusion, his mother was a Methodist and his father an Anglican, so he alternated between chapel and church until finally being nailed by the Anglicans.

After serving with the Royal Engineers, he golfed his way through Durham University, and started teaching Geography deep in the Fen district in September 1955. Promoted to a Southampton comprehensive school, he continued this, until changing circumstances resulted in his studying Programmed Learning at Birmingham University.

Moving to a local Catholic College of Higher Education, and finally to Southampton University, he ended an unbroken teaching career of some forty-seven years in November 2002, having taught colleagues at every level from nursery to Master's degree, and from an enormous range of different professional and curriculum backgrounds.

All these experiences have left him with an abiding interest in how and why people think as they do, and an increasing conviction that Montaigne was right to insist that there is a need for faith and divine revelation to overcome the inherent limitations of human reason. A depressive, highly anxious introvert, he relies on Seroxat, expensive Islay malt whisky, reasonable golf, tolerant friends, and an extensive medical, dental, psychological and spiritual support team, to get him through this life. He is happily married to Susan and has a fine son, Jack, both of whom luckily know how to cope with him.

SOLDIERING WITH SAINT IGNATIUS

SOLDIERING WITH SAINT IGNATIUS

Jack Oakley

ATHENA PRESS
LONDON

SOLDIERING WITH SAINT IGNATIUS
Copyright © Jack Oakley 2004

ISBN 1 84401 365 0

First Published 2004 by
ATHENA PRESS
Queen's House, 2 Holly Road
Twickenham TW1 4EG
United Kingdom

Printed for Athena Press

A thirty-week yomp through
The Nineteenth Annotation Spiritual Exercises.

(October to May 2004)
Jack Oakley

ACKNOWLEDGEMENTS

To Susie, my wife, who got me to do these exercises, and whose faith I can never match.

My deepest thanks to Sister Margaret, friend, guide and tutor, who week after week raised her eyes from my pages, and stared at me enigmatically for some time, rather '…like stout Cortez, silent upon a peak in Darien…' before once more dissecting, discussing, commenting, in-filling, and enriching what I had written, and all in the most patient, calm and deliberate manner. God alone knows what she really thought, but I learned a lot.

INTRODUCTION

The gift of choice, of freedom, is the most tremendous gift that has been granted to humanity. If you desire to love and preserve it, there is only one way: you must unconditionally and in total submission give it back to God – and give yourself as well.

Naturally the gift is so tremendous that you want to keep hold of it. But if you yield to this temptation, and look with egotistical desire upon freedom of choice you will lose your freedom.

And your punishment will be this: you will be utterly confused...

Søren Kierkegaard: 'Reflections on Freedom'
The Journal 1850–1854

Well, I am confused – and always have been – about religion, faith, theology, philosophy, psychology, this life, the next life, the Solar System, the Galaxy, the Universe, Jesus and God.

My mother was a Methodist; my father an Anglican; my wife is a Catholic, and my friends range from pagans to Buddhists. I like some Jews, I dislike some Muslims, and I'm still not sure what I am. I am seventy-three and time is running out.

I want to be something though. I want to be a satisfactory Christian.

I've twice done the Journey of Faith, and this book recounts my thirty-week struggle with St Ignatius' Nineteenth Annotation Spiritual Exercises.

The title attracted me since I am no stranger to 'spiritual' exercise at the nineteenth hole at my golf club. I do not offer this book as an explanatory guide, heart-warming revelation, mind-blowing insight, or inspired spiritual text or anything so erudite and worthy. If anything it is simply a thirty-week diary of thinking about things which confuse me, and might confuse you.

If you find the thoughts offensive, banal, irritating, politically incorrect or just wrong – then tough! They were my thoughts, all genuine, and often ground out with great effort, when I could have usefully been doing the laundry.

But if like me, you are confused about some pretty fundamental issues and concerns, and these thoughts help in any way at all then I am happy for you.

And I am happy for me.

PS If you are more than curious how a thirty-week spiritual exercise programme is actually structured, suffice it to say that the foundation stone is the following book. *Draw me into your Friendship. The Spiritual Exercises.* (A literal translation and a contemporary reading.) by David L Fleming, SJ, publisher, The Institute of Jesuit Sources, Saint Louis, 1996

It is cleverly designed so that on each left-hand page one reads the literal translation of the Ignatian Spanish autograph by Father Elder Mullan, SJ and on the right hand page a contemporary reading crafted by Father D L Fleming, SJ.

A lot of other reading was involved as well, but this book was paramount, and copiously referred to.

Reflections... October 22nd

It would be unwise and unrealistic to expect any major changes so far.

Yet I am conscious of some shifts, maybe just a clarification or two of thought and ideas.

I've read and thought about Job. I could never see the argument of his three 'comforters' that he must have done something wrong to be so punished. He obviously had not. Anyway, I can't easily accept that a merciful loving God would so punish anyone so consistently for reasons of His own, though to avoid Job's trap I have to.

For I do see that Job's mistake was to think he could reason things out with God 'man to man', as it were. This shows a fundamentally flawed image of God, who remains omniscient, omnipotent, omnipresent, and though loving each one of us greatly, and prepared always to listen, remains totally in control of everything... 'moving in mysterious ways His wonders to perform.' Argument is therefore out; so is compromise; and so are deals. God rules, okay? As Newman says in his wonderful prayer, 'He knows what He is about.'

All the other readings so far express this central notion in a variety of ways.

Total submission to the will of God is called for, and total acceptance that despite everything that may befall us, God's love is unfailing. This is where it gets hard. Searching back through the course of your life for signs of God's love and help is fraught with problems.

i) There's the little matter of proof. When you yell for help, there's no clap of thunder, no heavenly voice, no magic carpet out of the hell you are in!

Millions of dead soldiers would attest to that.

ii) So maybe God's help in such cases is simply to get you out of this world and safely into the next, where you will never again know such agony. Maybe He draws the line at helping us in evil situations which are of our making, and not His. Maybe He weeps in sheer pity and exasperation at our monumental stupidity. Who could blame Him? Certainly not me.

iii) But in less extreme situations it seems on reflection help is at hand. Certainly in my life, in the bad times, deep reflection shows how many times someone or some event turned up which eventually got the engine started again, which one could not have predicted. So was it God? I certainly accept that He is much more likely to work through other human beings, since the only other way is through the medium of prayer by the afflicted person, and Job shows there's a learning curve there, before that works. But doubt remains. Were they just nice people? (One certainly was a non-believer, which poses a question: can God work through a non-believer even if he/she is unaware that such is happening? Answer – obviously yes.)

iv) So, there still remains the matter of proof. Should this matter? There's the shrewd aphorism 'I believe so I can understand beats I understand so I can believe' which I have always suspected was invented by a very smart Jesuit to head off the sceptical and scientifically minded. On the other hand *if* you could prove the existence of God, that would totally do away with the idea of faith, or in fact the need for it, and what a can of worms would open up down here with the rich and famous jockeying for position in the next world as well as this! I like the idea of faith without proof, because it's the only level playing field the poor and needy share with the rich and powerful.

v) So, proof doesn't matter. It's an emotional need not an intellectual one. It would be lovely to have it, but it's like a comfort blanket in reality. If you want to grow up, you have to do without it, for faith means going forward clad only with the conviction that one backwoods Jewish carpenter, two thousand years ago, was in fact the most glorious thing that ever happened to our benighted planet. Looked at like that, no wonder a life of faith is so simple on the one hand, and so complex on the other. No wonder it calls for total submission to the will of God. No human being could design anything so bizarre, and calling for such an intensely personal decision.

vi) I do not think I am there yet. But, I have some doubts as to whether anyone else is either. Faith is not a plateau. You don't arrive. It's a journey, and I find myself thinking that it's rocky and uphill, and sometimes you stub your toes and bleed, and sweat and ache as you climb. But once in a while you round the bend and you step aside from the path for a moment and you rest, and spread before you like a fantastic view is a vision of the glory of God, and the peace and friendship of Heaven. It's more than enough to keep you going, for there is certainly not much else in this world which matches it.

vii) It helps to know others have been there before you. I deeply admire the thoughts expressed in Newman's prayer 'God has created me to do Him some definite service,' which shows sublime submission to the will of God and supreme conviction that He knows what He is doing. I also read and reread Kierkegaard's wonderful essay on God and Humanity from *The Unchangeableness of God*. Here he stresses that complete obedience to God is the means of releasing yourself into God's care. They provide fine examples.

Reflections... November 3rd

I don't find too much trouble in giving an hour a day to these exercises.

In fact I think it is probably more as I tend to sleep fitfully at night, and take frequent rests (so-called 'power naps') during the day. At such times I frequently find myself chatting to God. I've always had trouble with the idea of 'chatting' to God, since it seemed a bit lèse-majesté at one stage, and last week's study of Job reinforced this; but having recognised and conceded that it can never be on other than a student/master basis I've gone back to it. Context matters, and there will always be formal occasions calling for a different response to Him.

This weekend my wife and I went to Mass/Holy Communion/Eucharist (their words not mine) by invitation at St Paul's Cathedral in London, and found it a most welcome and satisfactory occasion. It is rare we can celebrate together, and it was made even more pleasant for my wife as the celebrant was a woman and the servers male.

The male dominance of the Catholic Church I find merely tedious, but it is a real pain for many of my women Catholic friends. On the other hand, I find the prolonged concentration on homosexuality as an issue in my own Church extremely worrying, and applaud the Pope's unequivocal stand against it. It is sad, though, that such issues leave ecumenism a total dead duck in the water. It leaves mixed-marriage partners like my wife and myself totally dependent on understanding clergy if we wish to receive Communion together. (I explained this problem to the celebrant in St Paul's who said, 'Believe me, I understand. My husband is a Catholic!')

We shall make a point of revisiting St Paul's next time. Their attitude is a real beacon of light and very, very rare.

It seems appropriate that this week, with my own Church seemingly about to break up, that 'sin' seemed to be the topic along with forgiveness. I must confess that I do not like the word 'sin'. I was brought up with the idea that the only time you used it was in connection with 'living in sin'.

My parents' generation used to whisper the phrase, usually accompanied by knowing glances, much clucking, and the odd giggle. So for me it will always have a prurient, itchy, sexual connotation. As far as I can see half the population is still 'living in sin' and not worrying about it, and at least forty per cent of children are good honest bastards, and we no longer care, though Heaven knows what the inheritance laws are now! It's a worry, not so much for the 'sin' as for the effect on children of unstable parental relationships; but it is a very old problem, and is unlikely to go away.

I am happier with the word 'error'. 'Forgive us our errors' makes much more sense to me (though you can't say 'as we forgive those who error against us' too easily.)

I make and have made lots of errors – many trivial, some serious – and the odd one very serious, to the point where one starts to worry about its effect. Such errors always cause damage to other people, either directly or indirectly, and probably have the same effect on oneself.

That is why forgiveness is vital, and we need God to forgive us so that we can eventually forgive ourselves, perhaps. The readings make it clear He is always eager to do so, so maybe it is down to the Protestant ethic, when you do not feel totally absolved, and the errors haunt you still!

Reflections... November 9th

I have found this week quite hard in one sense. It was not hard to understand the readings, or to think about them individually. What was hard was to put them all together and consider them as a whole. There simply did not seem to be any coherent pattern; or if there was, it was not one which brought a lot of comfort, but instead raised some very worrying questions.

We see in the readings expressions of the following ideas.

- Total submission to the will of God: Gen 12, Lk 1, Deut 6, Jn 3.

- The need to give up absolutely everything at whatever cost if you truly wish to be a follower of Christ. Mt 13. Mk 10, Deut 6.

- The rewards of so doing are enormous: total freedom (Lk 9), and the joy of living in God's love which is not earned by any of the foregoing actions, but is simply given by Him. (Which in itself is a little odd.)

- The resultant is to be prepared in some way to be truly a servant of Christ; to be able to hear, respond to, and carry out the work he wishes you to do.

What broke away from this pattern was Deut 6. In fact I got so involved that I read most of Deuteronomy, and for me a very different kind of God emerged. It was not so much a case of 'I'd like you to do this' but more 'If you don't do this then watch out!' The Ten Commandments rather faded into insignificance compared to all the other 'don'ts' that exist in Deuteronomy – for most of which, transgression results in death. I also thought that the people other than the Israelites got pretty short shrift. They either had to get out of Canaan, or it was quite okay to destroy them, and you could not help but feel sorry for Moses who, after all his work, leadership, trials and tribulations, was quite firmly told he would not be going to Canaan because of some earlier transgression.

This seemed to me a very scary sort of God. Not so much encouraging the points bulleted above, but downright insisting on them and then some, and Heaven help you if you failed – because He would not! I started thinking about primitive gods such as the Inca gods, who needed bloody sacrifices to placate them, and the Greek and Roman gods, who were just as quixotic, volatile, bitchy, treacherous, and unpredictable.

Since it would be a strange Christian who believed God was still like this, when did it all change? Who changed it? Do the Jews still believe in an Old Testament God? Since He told them in Deuteronomy they would always have to struggle against their enemies, it seems a bit like it. One could make a strong case that they still endure huge punishments at frequent intervals, so do they still keep annoying him? Why doesn't He punish Christians in the same way?

Perhaps he does and we don't quite ascribe it to him: war, pestilence, AIDS, famine etc. Perhaps the softer demands for total submission above are just that… softer demands rather than the old divine threats, but the concept is the same.

So I came out of it confused: trying to come to terms with all these different ideas and contradictions; hoping against hope that trying to believe in and trust in a loving God was the right way, was acceptable to Him, and that following Christ's two laws was what He wanted. I just want to look after my family and live in peace with my neighbours, and I'm worried that somehow this is not enough for Him.

Reflections... November 14th
(Principle and Foundation 23)

The first reflection is that the original statement (presumably written by Ignatius) is much easier to understand than the modern version, which I found much less crisp and somewhat more circumlocutory.

Ignatius does not feel the need to argue or elaborate or even defend his views too much. He states them almost as a series of unarguable axioms, and in toto they represent a clear recipe or programme:

1. Man was created solely to serve God, and thereby save his soul.

2. Everything else on earth exists simply for man to use in pursuit of this objective.

3. Choice is called for by man, since 'everything else' could either help or hinder the pursuit.

4. The 'hindrance' lies in the fact that certain things chosen by man, might in themselves become so attractive and involving, that they deflect man in his fundamental pursuit. In effect, they become 'ends' in themselves.

5. He must therefore cultivate 'indifference' to the appeal of such choices, and see them all as merely possible means to the 'end for which he was created'.

6. His choice will therefore always be determined by the degree to which that chosen, helps him to serve God and save his soul.

   All else will be ruthlessly discarded.

By contrast, the modern translation rambles on a bit about God's gifts, and becoming good stewards in our care for the world etc.,

etc. It seems to be almost written by a member of the Green Party. I can't help thinking that had Ignatius read it, he would have regarded all this as one of the 'hindrances', and his response would have been robust. 'Damn the environment, let's get back to God!' would, I suspect, have been close.

I find Ignatius impressive. His thesis is crystal clear; delivered without any kind of waffling about; is impressively rational; and possesses a kind of harsh, cold, adamantine and masculine quality which obviously reflects his time as a soldier.

Its strong axiomatic flavour is certainly the end product of a long period of experience, growth, study and reflection, resulting in the kind of unswerving conviction which gives rise to such statements.

The problem is an old one: that perpetual fine line between bigotry – or better still in the case of Ignatius and Paul, zealotry – and what the rest of we poor mortals can manage. We will always need the zealots carrying the banners and beating the drums. That is their function, and without them exhorting, chivvying, praising, chastising, teaching ad nauseam ad infinitum, the rest of us would probably remain virtually soul dead. I find myself being chivvied by the pair of them, not unwillingly so, but feeling there are limits to what I can do.

For example, I do not feel overtly 'hindered' by work, the desire for money or possessions, or the pursuit of some interest. I have no interest in cars, clothes, cruises, or the latest gizmo on offer. I have enough and more for my needs, thanks be to God, and my wants are usually few. I think I could give up my golf and swimming if I had to. Most of my friends and family are dead, and status and reputation are long since things of the past. My 'hindrances' are tied up with health and the need to stay alive for a little longer to see my son firmly on his way to adult life and an independent existence, and to give both my wife and my son whatever they get from my continued presence.

I would find it very hard if a stroke or other illness deprived me of the capacity to read and think.

Thus I am worried that both Ignatius and Paul seem to imply that I ought to be prepared to give all this up as well, if it impedes my approaching God, and imperils my soul; though Fleming rather comfortingly seems to suggest that our 'indifference' can sometimes be tempered by our 'responsibilities', and I certainly feel responsible for both my wife and my son.

So there I think I stand at the moment. I admire Ignatius as I say, and it is impossible not to admire Paul. They have much in common, and do not need commentators to translate and interpret for them. I find that gets in the way, and anyway as an academic I can't get out of the habit of reading such stuff with a view to marking it. (Arrogant maybe, but a professional habit!)

Since 'understanding is not achieving' – according to the handout – and 'achieving' is the gift of God, possibly helped by prayer, I can only press on and see what the good Lord decides. As Newman said, 'He knows what He is about.'

Reflections... November 25th

This week I have had considerable difficulty with the ideas and concepts put forward, and found myself questioning, in particular, the views put forward by Fleming, which I found less and less acceptable.

To begin with I have always thought the stories of the 'fall of the Angels' and Adam and Eve to be no more than charming stories. Stories with a strong moral point, but stories none the less. I can quite believe that Ignatius, given his time and particularly his place, would think otherwise and regard them as verities. But we know differently now.

It is most unlikely that Homo Sapiens descended from just two people, and it is even more unlikely that they would display the logical and verbal skills of Adam and Eve, should this be even remotely the case. So what we have are two Old Testament parables, which make a conventional moral point that evil can often result from poor choices.

I have no problem with this concept, and I readily concede that in such cases one apologises profoundly to God, and does all one can to put the matter right, asking for His understanding and forgiveness of our human frailty. Adam and Eve and Lucifer don't appear to have had the chance, and back we come to the 'one strike and you are out' God of the Old Testament, who as we know is more the construct of the writers than anything else. Definitely a case of, 'I've set it up like this for your benefit. Step out of line and you are out!' They did, and they were.

What I take further exception to is Fleming's language and obsession with sin. He really does come out as right over the top. He poses the question as to what we deserve with all our sins, when the Angels and Adam and Eve only committed one sin, which uneasily seems to imply the God of the Old Testament. He says, 'Out of me... so much evil, hatred and death can come forth.' Again, 'Myself... a sewer polluting the waters of the river of life... a walking contagion of diseases who continues to walk throughout the world affecting it and everyone who comes into my life.' I should not 'subtly seek for ways to escape and relieve the awfulness of sin which may be building up within me.'

I must not laugh too much, as 'laughter can be the attempt to escape from the uneasiness of the situation'. He is pretty much in favour of penance of one sort or another, even suggesting that flogging oneself 'coming down through our Christian tradition still may give direction to profitable forms of bodily penance today'. Sadomasochism lives, okay?

No! No! No! This is emotive language, and really out of touch with the humdrum lives that most people live. What on earth do you have to do to be 'a sewer polluting the waters of the river of life'? Maybe a combination of matricide, patricide, blasphemy, rape, incest, and sodomy – plus a modicum of genocide – might do it. But the odd lie, lapse of good taste, broken promise, selfish act, pride, arrogance and thoughtlessness towards God and your neighbour? I don't think that qualifies somehow, and that is what most people's sins amount to in my experience.

There is also one huge danger in all of this. It is never a good idea to tell people that they really are much more bloody awful than they thought they were. They start to believe it. In school, after I was fortunate enough to be properly retrained by guys who understood these things, I never 'punished'. I hunted high and low for anything I could praise, reward, or over-praise. People do not learn from their mistakes, they get scarred by them. But, they do appreciate all the praise they can get, even if it sticks in your throat to give it sometimes.

I can not believe that the good God operates in a totally different way, or demands the kind of quivering, abject, wilting, self-punishing object that seems to come out of Fleming's ideas. Taken to extremes, some of his ideas and concepts could reduce a less than robust stable personality to all kinds of psychiatric problems.

When I talk to God I make the greatest effort not to lie. To start with, there is only ever Him and me, and He knows very well when I am lying. So why bother? What I worry about is whether I do not know I am lying, but He does. If I have screwed up in some way, then while talking to Him about it I find it is impossible to get away with it. I get feelings of unease, guilt, sadness, and I know I have to try to do something to retrieve the situation. But it is positive, not negative. Action is called for somehow, not just lying there all covered in shame or something. I see no point in that at all.

'Shame' needs watching. I am often ashamed of being a member of the human race. I feel shame for other people whose behaviour at times is quite unbelievable and unacceptable. I have felt much shame as a result of other people's actions towards me. But I try to avoid situations leading me to feel it about my own actions. It all too often is an end in itself for a damaged personality, not a stimulus to do better.

So it's been a tough week. I have probably gone backwards. But there is no point in putting down anything other than what I feel. I hope my life is not too sinful. I do not think it is. It seems too humdrum and ordinary somehow. I think I know most times when I have slipped up, and I try to do something about it, even if tardily. That seems much more profitable than walking round trailing clouds of sin and guilt behind me. But as usual I could be wrong, but I genuinely feel Fleming needs to get out a bit more...

More Reflections… December 1st

Catching a glimpse inside a London church on television recently, which was obviously a centre for the black community, and noting the splendid rhythmic singing and clapping, and the general air of pleasure, happiness and liveliness which seemed part of this act of worship, I could not help but contrast it with some of the services I have attended in both Catholic and Anglican churches.

I have staggered out of some Masses so depressed and knouted by the general air of gloom, despondency, and the evident angst of the priest, that it took a stiff whisky before I could recover and face up to the world again. Likewise, a 7 a.m. Holy Communion Service in Bath Abbey was so bleak, cold and under-attended that it almost put my wife off joining me in my Church for life: a bit like reading the Riot Act to a bunch of mutinous troops.

Yet it was no surprise, really, since I was brought up to realise that only the very old and frail could hope to receive communion after 8 a.m. on Sundays, since getting up early was regarded by the Church as a subtle form of penance, Sunday being the only day of the week you could hope to have a lie-in. Miss it, and I frequently did, both as altar server and later on, and one brought down the wrath of the vicar with the inevitable set of totally negative feelings.

Ploughing through a second week on sin did little to change my view that Ignatius overemphasises it, and I am beginning to wonder whether the historic Spanish and Irish influence on the Catholic Church has much to answer for. Neither nation figures highly in the 'happy-clappy' stakes, and I can not for the life of me see either replicating in church the atmosphere that the West Indians can create.

When you begin to wonder why this is so, back you inevitably come to sin and guilt. How can you possibly be happy, when you barely get any respite from having to consider how sinful you are, despite a blameless week of shopping, ironing, housework, and worrying about the kids and the mortgage, and generally try to stay out of trouble, and avoid causing it for anyone else?

I was supposed this week to reflect on how 'my unlovingness spreads an atmosphere of anxiety and unhappiness wherever I go'. I had to picture myself as an 'infectious person' or a 'car's exhaust' to become 'more aware of the insidious spreading out of the effect on others of my unlovingness'. (Course Handout. Week 5.)

What I found myself reflecting on instead was the state of mind of the person who wrote this, particularly the metaphor of the 'car's exhaust', which any Freudian would regard as very significant, and indicative of somebody not too far perhaps from the anal stage of psychosexual development. It is quite possible to get so wrapped up in contemplating sin and guilt that you never contemplate anything else. Having contemplated it rather deeply for two weeks, I am having to fight the growing conviction that some Churches have got Christianity all wrong, or at least they have allowed individuals with their own problems too much sway in determining what matters.

God loves us; He has forgiven us our sins through the sacrifice of His beloved son; He wants us to acknowledge this in every aspect of our daily lives, and to work hard to avoid further sinning, not just use our eternal gifted forgiveness as a carte blanche for a general life of laissez-faire debauchery.

Christ does not seem ever to have made a song and dance about sin, loading on the guilt and the never-ending burden. Time and again he simply listens, tells an offender they are forgiven, and asks them not to re-offend. A clean slate, easy instructions to comprehend, a clear course of action – so get on and do it, and that is where the crunch comes, as Christ well knew. He does not endlessly rabbit on about being a walking infection, or spreading miasma about like the rear end of a goat. It's the Old Testament prophets who do that, laying on the burden until the mind is numbed by the repetition.

Likewise, I reflected that there was not a lot of point in contrasting all my difficulties (loving, forgiving, devaluing myself, timidity, lack of initiative etc., etc.,) with God's amazing capacities. He is God, omniscient, omnipotent, omnipresent, alpha and omega, and I am simply me. Why on earth would I want to carry out such a 'compare and contrast' exercise? I think I know the differences, and I also know that my estimate of the differences is likely to be so wide of the mark as to make God smile at my naivety and lack of understanding.

So I'm sorry, but I think I have had enough of contemplating guilt and sin, and having to try to cheer myself up after a particularly depressing Mass. I'm glad to have found a priest who recently invited everyone to a special Midnight Mass to celebrate England's winning of the World Rugby Cup. He was joking – the congregation knew he was – and everybody laughed. What a lift! What a relief! His enormous love of God and people, so obvious to all, was in no way compromised, and he knew God would enjoy the joke.

I did contemplate the seven deadly sins though for a while. I decided for me they probably descended from pride (quite high, since I like to think of myself as an above average teacher); anger (easily stoked by child murderers, suicide bombers, greedy capitalists, biased thinkers, Channel Four;) envy (not much, and mainly focused on people who achieve success easily. In my family we have a saying, 'If an Oakley wants anything he has to go to the gates of hell to get it!' This reflects the general sins of lying, devaluing, pessimism, cynicism and general bloody-mindedness.); lust (long ago and far away); greed (probably only for books); gluttony (No. I'm slimming.); and sloth (No. I'm a nervous workaholic.)

So, armed with this self-analysis, I shall continue to try to head off instances, and try to repair the damage when I fail to do so. But I think it a sin to keep contemplating sin, so I think it is time to move on and contemplate some of the joys of being a Christian. I'm a bit envious of people who can sing like those West Indians can. Not even the Welsh Chapels I occasionally went to, belting out 'Bread of Heaven', quite matched it.

I will also try to stop thinking of some Spanish and Irish Catholics as superstitious, touchy, cantankerous, priest-ridden Christians trailing clouds of incense, sin and guilt. But at the moment it's a strong image.

Reflections... December 8th

Well, this week it has been a relief to get away from contemplating sin, as it was beginning to get me considerably disturbed and irritated. I can see the value of being so disturbed, and do not object, but as I said last time there is the danger of some people being rendered incapable of acting in a positive way by such contemplation, and simply remaining 'shell-shocked in sin', as it were.

This does not seem to be a very valuable or life-giving exercise, though acknowledging errors and seeking forgiveness for them, and then moving on, certainly is.

Forgiveness itself is obviously a positive concept. It definitely allows 'moving on', since it closes some kind of negative event or experience. 'I forgive you,' obviously shuts down something; writes *Finis* to something which was acting negatively between persons, or even between whole groups of people or nations.

There are problems in pinning down exactly what it is, however.

A hunt through a thesaurus is enlightening. We find:

To forgive...   pardon, reprieve, amnesty.
Forgiven...   pardoned,   absolved,   shriven,   unresented, unavenged, unpunished, venial, excusable.
Forgiving...   placable,   condoning,   unresentful,   forbearing, long-suffering, patient.

From this roughly emerges the idea that the one sinned against pardons the act which caused the harm or suffering, almost admitting but perhaps not quite, that it never happened, while remaining unresentful, condoning, and placable. (It seems to me that to be forbearing, patient, and long-suffering are all prerequisites to being forgiving anyway.)

The forgiven person (the sinner) is now absolved, shriven and excused, and need not fear any form of punishment, revenge, or permanent blot on his/her record. The slate is to all intents and purposes wiped clean, as if nothing had ever taken place.

Contemplating all of this, it is again immediately obvious that God is the only one who can carry out this process as it should be carried out, particularly the 'deletion from the record' aspect. I know that various Christian sects still hold that somehow He and the angels tot up all your sins in a little black book, and that eventually there will be a dire reckoning, but again this seems to hark back to the God of the Old Testament. (Without wishing to be flippant, one only hopes modern Christian theology is right about God being a very loving, forgiving Father, otherwise some of us are in for a very nasty time later on!)

However, I doubt very much whether we poor humans can aspire to match God in the act of forgiveness. To start with, my personal experience and learning rather leads me to favour Freud's ideas that we have an id, ego, and superego.

The superego (or conscience) nags us to forgive, since if we have internalised the Christian message at all this is where it will reside, and it is the function of the superego to pressure the ego to do something about it. The ego (or realist) will generally try to obey the superego if only to relieve the pressure, or because it reflects pragmatically that if it doesn't forgive, it might not get it itself when it needs it. (A good Gallic thought process if somewhat cynical.)

Lurking below both the superego and the ego is the id, that 'child' of the personality and powerhouse of all psychic energy. Now the id obeys nothing but its own feelings, which can be quite violent. It has no morality. If it is damaged, insulted or sinned against, it screams, and it does not forget... ever... and it craves getting its own back. This is the problem.

It is quite possible that the ego, driven by the superego, will announce loud and long that it forgives, all is pardoned, let's move on etc., and it will even try to suppress in all kinds of ways the fact that the id is screaming in the background that it does *not*, forgive.

But the fact remains that it may all be a sham. If the ego does too good a job of suppression it is not unknown for this to cause all sorts of other problems (e.g. an addiction to alcohol, in the case of a dead friend), which might have been alleviated if an inability to forgive had been admitted in the first place.

So here is a very good source for all kinds of problems, and I can't escape the thought that Christianity is responsible for some of them. I can study the parable of the Prodigal Son many times, but I have always had awkward thoughts. The father seems to me, by his actions to be unbelievably forgiving, and I can accept this only as a metaphor for God. Having seen half his capital dissipated by the younger son (who returns basically only because he is hungry) seems to leave him totally unaffected, which stretches the boundaries of credibility for a human too far in my opinion. Likewise his treatment of the elder son, has always struck me as a little indifferent to say the least, and I suspect the elder son would remain in a decidedly unforgiving mood. But as a parable for the actions of God forgiving even if repentance is a bit iffy, it remains enormously comforting which is presumably how Christ meant it. To err is human and to forgive like this divine.

But for us poor humans? I don't think we can always do it for the reasons stated above. I think we can sometimes suffer great guilt and damage when we contemplate the fact that we *can't* do it. This again strikes me as an unnecessary burden to carry, since we are not divine. Neither do I like the idea that we carry out all kinds of sublimations or displacements to disguise the fact that we can't do it.

Far better to be honest, surely, and admit our current inability to measure up? Or does that now worry us further, as it might bar us from Heaven? Caught between the id and the devil is no place to be.

There is one further problem. In the parable the father (i.e. God by inference) forgives *before* he has even been asked to do so. He sees the son 'far off' and is moved to pity. If the son subsequently asks for forgiveness, he does it in a pretty roundabout way.

'I have sinned against Heaven and against you,' is more a statement of the offence, rather than a request for forgiveness. So it looks a bit like God grants forgiveness before it is asked for, and possibly even in the case when the sinner is not actually going to ask for forgiveness, either out of pride, contempt for the injured, total indifference, or psychosis. How many humans can match that?

I would have (and actually do have) great difficulty in forgiving, if the person who injured me does not even try to ask for some forgiveness. Does that score a black mark against me? I hope not, because surely forgiveness is a reciprocal process for humans, if not for God?

But there is one strategy which seems worthwhile and offers a little hope that we can escape from these dilemmas, which is to 'walk in the moccasins' of the sinner and try to see things from his point of view. I have no problems with this, *unless* by implication I am expected always to come up with a benign or positive excuse for the sinner.

This again seems to me to stretch human goodness to unacceptable limits. If after long thought and walking in the moccasins of the sinner I arrive at the final conclusion that 'X really was an unmitigated evil swine', or 'Y really was a sociopathic misfit', or 'Z really was an immoral treacherous trollop', I can accept and value the strategy because the findings might be true, (human beings being what they are) and the strategy at least offers me some kind of reason to reduce the pain and scar of my injury.

But if I feel a sort of 'Christian pressure' to twist things so that the action which damaged me so badly always has to be seen in some way as perfectly pardonable, reasonable and acceptable when seen from the sinner's point of view, then I start to feel I am being manipulated again, and this time manipulated unfairly.

So there are again no easy answers this week, just the problem of seeing what God can do, and knowing we can never match it, but struggling to do the best we can. I have not really resolved the problem of facile forgiveness, just established the fact that it exists, and that I am uncertain whether it is more meritorious to refuse to do it, or more pragmatic to claim success; not that I see much point in the latter, since God can spot a sham better than anyone else. However, there does seem a little merit in putting on the moccasins of the sinner now and again, providing after long and careful and dispassionate thought I am not debarred from finally reflecting what a prize bastard he or she was, because it could always be true.

Reflections… December 15th

This week the concern has been 'structural sin'. Structural sin is defined as:

> The sin of a corporate group of people, who benefit at the expense of another group, by wielding power over it, oppressing it, or impoverishing it in one way or another.
>
> A group is committing structural sin when it is being unjust to another group, and the injustice has become institutionalised, part of the fabric of life, part of the culture of the group, unreflectively taken for granted. Possibly today, for most 'good' people, their worst sins are not their personal sins, but their involvement in structural sin.

I have no problems with the definition of structural sin. I have no problems with the dynamics either. One could regard the whole of human history, in any place, at any time, as a record of how one group has been unjust to another group, and the injustice has been institutionalised by those in power. In fact structural sin seems to be the first and most obvious outcome of the acquisition of power, political, military, social, economic, spiritual, or psychological. One thinks of the slave states of the Romans and Greeks; the feudal system; the Inquisition; the industrial revolution; the autocracy of the Tsars; Hitler; Pol Pot; and Saddam; the list is endless, and shows absolutely no signs of stopping.

But as usual there is a problem. The columnist Peter Simple, who used to write a humorous column for the *Daily Telegraph* entitled 'The Way of the World', had a spoof psychiatrist called Dr Heinz Kiosk, who would pronounce eruditely, lengthily, and politically correctly on every world problem under the sun, and would always send his audience screaming for the exits by finishing hysterically, 'We are *all* guilty!'

I found Dr Kiosk entering my mind immediately I read the

opening sentence on the handout Structural Sin (1) 'Once I realise my complicity in structural sin...'

Now 'complicity' is a very awkward word to use in the context of 'structural sin'. Complicity means a ready willingness to enter into an evil act. Complicity actually implies a *partnership* in an evil act. So I have apparently to consider that I am playing a 'ready, willing and able' role in structural sin in one or all of its forms.

Then I have to consider all its forms. Slavery, apartheid, ethnic cleansing, the treatment of women, the impoverishment of the Third World, inner city deprivation, homelessness, homophobia, jingoism, anti-Semitism, racism, totalitarianism, corruption in all its forms, pollution of virtually everything, terrorism, the exploitation and extinction of animals etc., etc. *Wow*!

I've even got a problem making sure that I haven't missed an example of structural sin. In fact, one of few engaging aspects of the whole structural sin bit, is waiting to see which new structural sin someone dreams up next...

So, not only do I have to bear the guilt of all my own individual sins, but I have to cope with an additional load of structural sins. No wonder some people find it all too hard to bear, or simply turn away and ignore the whole idea, or get relief like Heinz Kiosk by yelling 'We are all guilty!' and go round reminding you of *your* share in the hope that it reduces *their* load somewhat.

Studying anthropology as an undergraduate, I was most taken by a tribe who lived in Chota Nagpur in India. They had institutionalised structural sin to the extent, that their only real topic of conversation was how unhappy and unworthy they were. This was actually a very clever defence mechanism they had worked out, since they thought that if they ever confessed to being happy or well-off their gods would immediately punish them.

I have a feeling that this lurks about a bit with some Christian sects and is maybe linked in with the God of the Old Testament again.

So it pays to be a bit more analytical, as it usually does. There are some structural sins I obviously know nothing at all about, since they are in other places and other cultures. There are some in other cultures, to which I might object strongly (such as the Afghans' treatment of women), but to which I do not think I have the right to object in any forceful way, since I do not live in their country and was not born in that culture. If the Afghans choose to live in my country, yet pursue such behaviours, I consider that a different matter, since I feel to persist in such behaviours is to interfere in *my* culture. (The British Army, having recruited lots of Fijians, is now quietly having to tell them that regular wife-beating is not allowed in our culture, though it is in theirs.)

There are some structural sins which I might have to accede to simply because they are put in place by a powerful political or economic system. I might be too much of a coward to risk my life or that of my loved ones to object, though one knows of countless people who did just that and died as a result. One merely has to think of Nazi Germany.

One could always fly from such a system if one had the money and means as many did, but for many that is not an option. One thinks of those Africans trapped in Zimbabwe, who are not of Mugabe's tribe. Likewise capitalism has many structural sin aspects to it, but willy-nilly I have to live with it unless I choose to go and live in Cuba, which is to swap one structural sin system for another.

There are some structural sins I can obviously totally avoid, once I recognise them for what they are. I do not have to be racist; I do not have to be fascist; I do not have to be anti-Semitic; I do not have to be against the equality of women. Avoiding them is very often the result of education, but one has to admit that context and experience are key variables.

It is much easier to be accepting of immigrants if one lives in a nice expensive middle-class area where it is most unlikely that immigrants will settle. I saw for myself the problems that working-class people in the West Midlands, initially very welcoming, faced when thousands of West Indians and other groups moved in during the 1950s. Particularly irritating to the local steel workers was the ease with which their Pakistani workmates could keep replacing their wives with one or more younger models. Most infuriating!

There are many structural sins which I can't hope to destroy, but which I can keep chipping away at, in the hope that if enough of us do it, some major reform might take place. One has the example of apartheid in South Africa, and the 'Free Mandela' campaign as a beacon. So what dealing with structural sin seems to boil down to in my opinion is something like the following:

1. Watch the 'We are all guilty! syndrome. In many cases you are not, and it is ridiculous posing that you are, going around like a demented *Guardian* reader, full of angst but short on logic.

2. Sort out the things that you can do nothing about, and are best left to the people on the spot who understand the ramifications and the implications (like the fact that tinkering with the water supply is upsetting the Aral Sea). Then forget them.

3. Sort out the things you can do something about into some form of priority, then choose the ones which have most significance or appeal for you. Do not be afraid to eliminate. You are not God, and you can't cover everything. Besides, if He feels you are missing something He will surely tell you.

4. Formalise your help in some way, if it means you can then save time dealing with some issue. It is easy to make out standing orders for your charity-giving for example; or to list the charity demands you look for in the post. I support Mind, Sense, Botton Village, Mencap, Sightsavers, the Lifeboats and the Gurkhas. The rest go straight into the bin unopened.

5. It is possible to join groups who carry out specific actions. I am a bit limited in this, and could possibly extend things in this area.

6. It is always possible to write letters. I have recently had two published concerning Southampton University and age discrimination, and the suspicious deaths of young soldiers at Deepcote Barracks. It may only alert people to the fact that a problem exists, but it is a miniscule something. It is now very easy to e-mail anywhere in the world.

7. Writing letters means of course that you are aware of the problem, which implies you need to read, watch, listen and stay alert. But it also means that you have to get rid of the 'It is

nothing to do with me', or 'I can't be bothered' attitude, which means changing to, 'Hang on! This perhaps is something I need to consider.'

8. It also means talking to and listening to God. Very often he slips the odd disturbing thought into your conscience, and you won't get any peace until you have done something about it. Which is what He intended.

So, perhaps finally the way to tackle structural sin is not to run around following Heinz dementedly yelling 'We are all guilty of it!' but to think, calmly and dispassionately, 'I am capable of doing something, however small, about this' – and then doing it.

Reflections… Christmas week.
December 22nd

This week was a bit of a paradox. I did not get too much that was new out of the basic idea for the week, and again found myself contemplating the times and pressures on Ignatius when he was writing this. I think what started the train of thought was the remark, 'It is my will to conquer all the land of unbelievers.'

For Ignatius in Spain, the knowledge of the Moorish conquest must have been quite sharp and the clash of religions something deeply bedded in, rather like Northern Ireland of the present day. With memories of El Cid and Roland and Oliver, and his knightly background, one can quite easily see where he got the idea from of a powerful king looking for followers for a great quest. But the twentieth century is a far less impressionable age. Many of us, and I count myself firmly amongst these, are deeply suspicious of charismatic leaders.

We have had a gut full of them. In my lifetime, for example, there have been Mussolini, Franco, Hitler, Stalin, Pol Pot, Idi Amin, Ho Chi Min, Mao, Saddam, Mugabe, etc. etc., ad nauseam.

Even when they don't turn out to be homicidal psychotic maniacs they can still be deeply flawed and capable of objectionable behaviours either personal, social or political. One thinks of Kennedy, Thatcher, Clinton, Berlusconi, etc. I have a profound distaste for and suspicion of anyone who decides he is worthy of being put into some position of power over the rest of us, and I start looking immediately at 'what's in it for him/her?' As some wise old historian (Lord Acton) said, 'Power corrupts, and absolute power corrupts absolutely.'

I always had a soft spot for Nero, another example of power gone crazy, who at least had the insight to note openly that given the chance, everybody would be just as corrupt as he was. The only one absolved from this is of course God, and through him, of course, Christ. Which is why I thought the comparison suggested by Ignatius, though a useful idea for less educated times, was fundamentally a bit iffy for today. I don't think the idea of a bunch of militant Christians galloping out to the 'lands of the unbeliever' is a good idea, whether the land is Africa, Asia, Bradford, Southall, or the West Midlands.

We have had all that in the last century and I well remember, as a student anthropologist, studying the devastating effect of some aspects of Christianity on African tribes. (Old widows were for example always taken on in some polygamous societies by some man, simply so that they could be kept alive. Come the Christian idea of 'one wife' only, they were only too readily left to starve, and a burden removed.)

It behoves us these days to be much more careful. The problem of course is when another faith has totally different ideas, one could even say 'is a bit more Ignatian that we are' and wants to gallop into *our* lands and convert *us* as unbelievers.

The more extreme versions of Islam have lots of charismatic leaders, all ready to do just that given the chance, which is decidedly worrying. So where does Christ fit into all of this? A charismatic leader… obviously.

A leader with a mission… obviously. A man who wanted followers… obviously. But it is when one ponders how He went about things that the huge differences between Him and all the other kings and leaders appear. To begin with His followers were not given material rewards, of the sort which other leaders tend to shower on their closest aides simply to keep them on side in most cases. Neither were dissidents and traitors firmly got rid of before they could cause real damage, viz. Judas.

Nothing was extracted from the people who listened to Jesus or were converted by Him; no taxes, party subscriptions, or whip-rounds at the end of the Beatitudes. He seemed to be content with whatever was provided for Him wherever He went, and often contributed more than He received (the wedding feast.)

When things approached the ultimate conclusion, which He knew was coming all along, there was no final fight or flight, no hiding in a hole in the ground and trying to negotiate terms. He even prevented His followers from drawing swords and fighting for Him, when the cops came.

He did not try to escape His terrible death, and even had the incredible patience and fortitude to ask forgiveness for His enemies and to try to comfort the two criminals dying with Him. Compare that with Hitler blowing his brains out, Mussolini running for it before he was shot, buried, dug-up and hoisted upside down on a lamp post, Kennedy shot down, Idi skulking in Saudi, and Saddam holed up in squalor. That's a very different kind of leadership.

For once I think Fleming's interpretation of Ignatius is better and certainly more in tune with the twentieth century, and he gets right to the core of what this new kind of leadership is.

He says Jesus' call goes out to all peoples, yet He specially calls each person in a particular and unique way. 'It is My will to win over the whole world, to overcome evil with good, to turn hatred aside with love, to conquer all the forces of death – whatever obstacles there are that block the sharing of life between God and humankind. Whoever wishes to join Me in this mission must be willing to labour with Me, and so by following Me in the struggle and suffering may share with Me in the glory.'

This is the leadership of subversion. It is directly antithetical to the kind of leadership with all the trappings of power that we are so used to, and so sick of.

It is not the giving of power to sick egotists with absolutely no capacity to use it wisely.

It is giving power to the serfs, the downtrodden, the inadequate; the truly little people.

It is saying, 'Listen! You. Yes – you! You really can make a difference in this world, by what you do with and to everyone around you. You may think you can't do much, but if we *all* do a little that is a *lot*. Millions of ants can shift a mountain. Follow My example and you will truly see God, and you can start the process *now* by moving closer to God in all you do.'

The problem is obvious. The little people are all too often told by the Big People that they need the Big People to look after them, and the poor little people keep believing it, until another few million of them get killed off following the Big People's 'leadership'.

It seems to be a very slow process in getting the little people to grow up. Education and learning to think for yourself is hard, often dull and ineptly taught, and it's easier to watch 'Pop Idol' (or maybe 'Pop Idle' is more apposite?).

The best we can say is that Christ started the process, and that it seems to be gathering a little strength as more and more people protest about more and more things. Our 'leaders' don't and won't ever like it for obvious reasons, which is why every Christmas we should hugely and loudly rejoice that possibly the best and most subversive of leaders comes into the world to remind us yet again of what real leadership is all about.

Post Christmas reflections...
January 5th, 2004

I must confess right at the start that I have a particular love-hate relationship with Christmas. Two very bad periods of my life in 1960 and again in 1966, both connected with the break-up of my first marriage, occurred exactly at Christmas time. On both occasions I had to go through the farce of appearing to be having a happy time, in order to keep two sets of parents both contented and in ignorance of the true state of affairs, knowing full well on the second occasion that things were finally over.

Looking back, I am surprised that I had the capacity to do it, but with hindsight I have come to appreciate that the damage done was both very deep and long-lasting.

For many years after, I tried to totally ignore Christmas. Living on my own made this very easy. One simply took no notice of the season, made very little preparation for it, lost oneself in work and other activities, and breathed a mighty sigh of relief when it was all over. Needless to say, going to Church or thinking about the real meaning of Christmas did not figure in things at all. January was a time of looking forward in some senses, and November was a time of real gloom when Christmas hung like a black shadow, something dreaded and something to be got through with as little grief as possible. I can't honestly say that these negative feelings have entirely disappeared, but what I can now say is that I genuinely feel they have apparently lost any real power to hurt. That has been quite a discovery.

It has not been easy to track back in time and memory to when the process of rehabilitation started, but this Christmas I have done a lot of thinking about it. I probably would not have done this at all had it not been for the Ignatian Exercises, fearing to arouse a lot of old demons. But having been asked to think a great deal about all the events surrounding the Birth of Jesus, I rapidly discovered that I was contemplating something like a three-strand electric cable and it was quite impossible to concentrate on the Birth of Jesus alone.

One strand was the actual Birth of Jesus; one was my past history of dreadful shattering Christmases; and one was the many happy Christmases I have since shared with my wife, son and friends. Finding it impossible, as I say, to concentrate solely on one strand, I just let my thoughts and feelings run themselves on all three strands to see where it led me.

The first long train of thought led me to the conclusion that for many people Christmas is not a happy time, and never has been. There are always the people who experience dreadful events at Christmas, and this Christmas has been no exception, with the usual clutch of wars, bombs, plane crashes, murders, road accidents etc.

A neighbour has just lost a much-loved sister over Christmas. Somehow it all seems that much worse when it occurs at this time. It is as if we want to cry, 'What are you doing, God, to let all this happen? Don't you know it is Christmas?'

Then there are always the old, poor, deprived, lonely, and dropouts for whom Christmas must be a doubly difficult time, since they see everyone else apparently having a much better time than they can hope for. But this, on deeper reflection, is because the real meaning of Christmas has been lost, and what we have instead is the surface glitz and gloss which is hyped up by the media, the press, the shops, the short sharp carol services, Santa Claus, the lights, people's false expectations, the whole schmaltzy package.

I found myself thinking about what it must have really been like for Mary and Joseph at Christmas time. Forced to ride out in winter, a pregnant woman on mule back, to Bethlehem at the whim of the occupying forces; stuck for anywhere reasonable to stay when they got there; camping out in some cold windswept stinking barn surrounded by rough animals; giving birth in grotesquely unhygienic and inappropriate conditions; and all the time wondering what would happen next.

Somehow the net result of this line of thought was to get well away from the image of 'Christmas *must* be a happy time' to the realistic idea that it is really no different to any other time as far as having lousy things happen, which I found oddly contenting.

This was when I saw more clearly that family sharing at Christmas is very fundamental. I know there are occasions when families have bitter rows at Christmas, but I can't help feeling that this is not caused by Christmas. The relationships have already broken down, and again trapped by the notion of 'Christmas *must* be a happy time', the problems are exacerbated.

But if the family relationships are fine, then Christmas is indeed a happy time. On reflection, I realised I had began to enjoy Christmas once again when I had to think much more about the needs of my new wife and young son than myself. Sharing Christmas with a young, growing and excited child is quite something else. This led inevitably to the third strand of the cable which was the Holy Family itself. Mary and Joseph went to Bethlehem *not* a family, but they became one, and a very special one. At that moment all the hardship of the journey, the poor surroundings, the pain and whatever lay ahead, all faded into insignificance. They must have been very, very happy.

For me then, it all synthesised into the conclusion that linking Christmas with bad times was really rubbish, that bad times can come at any time; that I had also been very fortunate in later having a loving and warm family and friends, and that my personal rehabilitation was due entirely to this, and had started much earlier than I had thought.

I also realised that I had started going back to church earlier than I had thought, and that, unconsciously maybe, thinking about Christmas had started then.

But it is only very recently that I began to contemplate what that first Christmas had probably really been like for Mary and Joseph. With all the cribs and shepherds and wise men there is more than a hint of smaltz, and it is easy to get trapped and stay trapped in the wrong image. You have to get through even this before you see the real significance of family love, and how Christ who experienced this as a child, then extended this to all of us for all time.

This leads inevitably to finally contemplating the nature of that special baby. No human baby, however loved, could extend love to all of us as Christ does. That takes a divine nature, and for God to send Christ to do it is the Christmas gift to end all Christmas gifts for all of us. Yet not everyone feels that love, and on occasions even the most devout do not feel it.

Feeling that love, enjoying to the full that gift, I now know imposes the need for us to remain a willing member of His family, and to work and struggle to follow Him, and I rather like the idea that that is our Christmas gift to Him, and one that He would appreciate. It's just that sometimes it is so hard to do.

Reflections... January 12th

This week the exercises have not been productive of any one dominant thought or idea. In fact several seemingly independent ideas have come to mind, all of which have been interesting to muse about, but everything seems to have been rather low-key after the much more significant and triumphalist events of the Birth of Our Lord and the celebrations of Christmas.

On reflection, though, I suppose Mary and Joseph experienced no more and no less of what every set of loving parents experience following a birth. First there is the excitement and worry of realising you are actually going to be parents (and in Mary's case this must have been greatly heightened by the realisation of the extraordinary demand that had been made upon her by God;) then there is all the preparation leading up to the birth; then there is the birth itself with all the consequent brouhaha; and then when the circus has left town there is a growing realisation that life will now never be the same, and you are in for a long and worrying haul in all kinds of ways, so you had better just get on with it since you do not have any other choice other than to run away, which sadly is not unknown.

No wonder young parents suddenly feel inadequate and bereft, and experience all kinds of depression and other negative feelings. I was a mature parent in a well-established job, able to afford all kinds of help and support, and yet I found being a parent of a young child a task which was fraught with all kinds of worries. It demanded the most enormous effort and commitment, which is only now beginning to ease slightly.

It's a pity in many ways that the Gospels tell us so little about the early life of Jesus. We know that Mary and Joseph went to the Temple in Jerusalem to give thanks and to make the obligatory offering. We know that they then returned to Nazareth where 'the child grew and became strong, filled with wisdom; and the favour of God was upon Him.'

We know that the family returned to Jerusalem every year for Passover, and that when Jesus was twelve He was left behind and not missed for a day, and then not found for a further three (which always surprises me, and makes one wonder if Mary and Joseph were not in some ways a bit negligent!).

We know He was a bit precocious in holding His own in discussion with the elders in the Temple, and even then appeared to be in some ways aware of His mission: 'Did you not know that I must be in my Father's house?'

Then the interesting details peter out: 'But He went with them to Nazareth and was obedient to them.'

Virtually twenty years then pass before we meet Jesus on the banks of the Jordan being baptised, and then of course all the Gospels give us all the details we could ask for about Him. But I think one would have to be less than human if one did not speculate about the 'missing' years.

I know there is the point of view which says that we have enough to do in absorbing His teaching and following His example without worrying about anything else. But we are taught that Christ came to us to share our humanity so that He could experience all that we experience, as well as experiencing, at the same time, His own especial relationship with God which no human can possibly experience and understand.

So it is almost impossible *not* to ask questions about what His childhood and adolescence were like, how He got on with His siblings and friends, what work and play He engaged in, what He did throughout the long period of His twenties when His contemporaries were establishing themselves in jobs and professions, getting married, and starting families etc.

It's as if Christ springs fully formed onto the world stage, rather like Athene from the head of Zeus.

However, I reached the conclusion that ultimately it did not matter, since we were never likely to find out, unless someone somewhere turns up another authentic Gospel.

It also does not matter for one other significant reason: whatever Christ was doing in those missing years it was time well spent. No one reading the accounts of His teaching can fail to be aware that He is a superb teacher, particularly of an illiterate uneducated population. His use of parable is unparalleled, and His capacity to make the point in simple language using a wide variety of experiences and concepts, well within the knowledge of His audiences, implies that He must have spent all those years in gaining and reflecting upon a wide range of experience, and in studying the skills and craft of a rabbi. It is interesting to compare His style with the involved and convoluted style often used by Paul, who presumably experienced all the good and bad bits of a Greco-Roman education system. One can recognise also that He must have spent long periods of solitary prayer with God, being made more and more aware, as He grew up, just what His mission involved.

It is quite impossible to imagine that such a mission was simply given to Him as a package or directive. If anything needed a long gestation period and extremely careful and potent nurturing, Christ's mission did.

The other train of thought this week was in some ways complementary to the idea of growing up. It was the idea of 'running down' or coming to the end of things. It was sparked off by Simeon's words, 'Lord, now lettest Thou thy servant depart in peace, according to Thy word: For mine eyes have seen Thy salvation…'

I have always loved the *Nunc Dimittis* (Luke 2), which I have always seen as a poem. I detest modern translations of it which destroy this. (It won't be long before some fool produces the ultimate in dumbing down: 'Look, Chief. It's time for me to pop off if You don't mind, now I've had a good butcher's at…' just so that the modish who seem to infest everywhere can get hold of it.) We also have the 84-year-old Anna, who 'spoke of the child to all who were looking for the redemption of Israel'.

There is something wonderful and majestic about Simeon. Told he would not die before he had seen the Lord's Christ, he simply knew when it was time to go to the Temple, and he simply knew this was the child. He takes the child in his arms and blesses God, and then simply and humbly makes his request to God.

But reading and thinking about it forces the realisation that it is all much deeper than this. We see that Simeon is absolutely aware that his life is now complete, Alpha has met Omega, the last sweet drop of wine has been drunk, the last bit of the jigsaw has fallen into place. The event he has been waiting for has happened and anything else would be an anticlimax and ultimately pointless. Not much good offering him thirty per cent off at the sales, or one more trip to Tesco's.

Yet it isn't a case of weltschmerz with Simeon, the sort that wipes out a lot of old people and certainly wiped out my own mother, who simply had had enough and could not be bothered to live any longer. Simeon's statement shows that he was well aware that, old as he was, God had really given him both a promise *and* a task.

That task was to wait patiently to see Christ and to bless God for what He had given the world, and Simeon was not going to fail in that task. Having completed it (and, one can guess at his enormous satisfaction in so doing), he asks for his just reward. One can't help but feel he does it in the spirit of a tired, exhausted, but very satisfied winner, who now simply wants to go home happily and confidently and enjoy his prize.

One only hopes God granted his request forthwith, because in my book he deserved it. It also left me envious of Simeon and Anna because one does not feel they were afraid of death either. It's as if the tasks they had to complete were actually interfering with their desire to die, and they could not go before they were completed.

This seems rather different to the present day, when we are advised to get heavily involved in self-appointed tasks to help us prolong mental and physical life and so put off death.

This prompted the final thought that for Anna and Simeon belief in the goodness of God was unquestioned. Faith was rock solid, not something that had to be struggled for. Also there is a kind of impressive fatalism and acceptance that life has a beginning and an end, a circularity and a completeness. We seem to have lost all that and given life a linear form, rather like an escalator, and the result is we are all rather afraid to get off. It would be no bad thing to concentrate on Simeon's example a lot more. I personally know I have a very long way to go before I get anywhere near his attitude.

Reflections… January 18th

There's been quite a lot to think about this week, and the readings have been interesting, particularly the long chapter from Hebrews, which I had never read before; which is really the stimulus for most of the thoughts that follow.

As I understand the purpose of Hebrews, it was a letter written to a group of Christians who, facing opposition and possibly persecution, were in danger of losing their faith. The writer encourages them by showing them that Jesus Christ is the true and final revelation of God. He emphasises three crucial truths:

1) that Jesus is the eternal Son of God, who learned true obedience to the Father, through the suffering He endured, and that as the Son of God He is superior to all the angels, prophets and Moses himself;

2) that God has declared Jesus to be our eternal priest, superior to any other; and

3) that as High Priest He alone provides the believer with salvation freeing him from fear, sin and death.

In Chapter 11 the writer carries out a lengthy review of the faith of some of the most important persons in Israel's long history, and appeals to his readers to remain steadfast in their faith. He goes on to urge them to endure whatever suffering and persecution may come to them, since it shows that 'God is treating you as his sons. Was there ever a son who was not punished by his father?' (Hebrews 12:7).

This led on to thoughts that Jesus would have learned much from his earthly father, Joseph. A lot of the other readings, particularly those from Deuteronomy, stress the importance of the Ten Commandments and the need for parents to make them known to their offspring at every opportunity and in every way. 'Teach them to your children. Repeat them when you are at home and when you are away, when you are resting and when you are working. Tie them on your arms and wear them on your foreheads as a reminder. Write them on the doorposts of your houses and on your gates.' (Deut 6:7–9.)

I'm quite certain that Joseph and Mary would have been the sort of parents to have done this, particularly Mary who would be more intimately aware of God's trust in her.

I found myself pondering the reaction of our modern population to anyone brave enough to repeat it. One occasionally sees the Ten Commandments still written on the walls of very old churches in faded letters, if the Church hasn't been turned into a restaurant, or a bijou block of flats, or a trendy community centre, in which last case they will probably have been whitewashed over. But I don't doubt that anyone posting them on his gatepost instead of 'Tuscany' or 'Kevan'Tracey' these days would immediately have a visit from irate neighbours, a Social Services' Counsellor, or more worryingly the Race Relations Board. (Tempora mutantur or Veritas odium parit?)

Jesus certainly had an early introduction to state interference. No sooner was he born than his parents had to run for it. Herod, as we know, displayed all the murderous paranoia that we have sadly come to expect from autocratic rulers, and having been thwarted of his prey, promptly took it out on a whole set of innocent bystanders – which is par for the course as far as autocrats are concerned. Something else occurred to me reading about the Flight into Egypt, and that was the question of distance. We blithely read about Mary and Joseph going from Nazareth to Bethlehem for the census in the middle of winter. Then we read about them flying from Bethlehem to Egypt, and in both cases as if it is just a stroll in the park.

In the first case it is at least 120 kilometres and in the second it is 250 kilometres to the Nile Delta and the towns of Egypt, assuming they did not stop in the desert somewhere. Then you must consider the state of the roads, the fact that it would have been on foot or mule back, the fact that the roads were by no means free from robbers, and the fact that Mary was in a delicate post-natal state and that

Jesus was a baby. It's not an overemphasis to state that for Him the introduction to suffering began very early indeed. Even when they finally came back, they could not go to Bethlehem but had to go right back up north to Nazareth and Galilee, and I'll bet there were a few sleepless nights even then wondering if the long arm of the new ruler was going to reach out for them. I did not feel there was much profit on speculating about the missing years of Jesus. Besides, the letter to the Hebrews had sparked a whole series of questions in my mind about the Jewish people. There are so many questions which emerge, so few real and convincing answers.

Why did God choose the Jews in the first place? Why not the Chinese or Indians – so much more developed and advanced at the time? Why do all the prophets dwell so much on sin, failure, and punishment, and why is the history of the Jews one of almost unbroken punishment, failure, struggle and persecution?

If ever a people have every right *not* to believe in God's love it is the Jews. If ever any family had to suffer the trials and tribulations of an unpredictable 'stick and carrot' Father it is them.

I know that much of the persecution they have endured since the Crucifixion is simply because many early Christians held them directly responsible for putting Christ to torture and death. Periodic slaughter of the Jews has taken place at many times and in many places since Christ's time, and the Holocaust was merely the latest and most extensive massacre. But one must not forget that religion alone is not responsible for this.

Christians have quite happily slaughtered Christians, and some of the Crusaders were the worst of all; though the long series of European Religious Wars, still unhappily continuing in Northern Ireland, run them a close second.

One other factor lies in the letter to the Hebrews and the writings of the Prophets. The Jews are a people brought up in an ocean of guilt. They almost drown in it. Very rarely are they allowed to forget their sins and transgressions; and in their case they pay for it bitterly and very frequently. Moreover they are told to endure it at whatever cost, because they will eventually be rewarded. Submission to rulers and authority was always drummed into them.

One surprising fact demonstrating this occurred in captured Russia during the war. The SS execution squads put up notices telling all Jews to report to the railway station in one province, and were absolutely overwhelmed by the numbers who did. This is a vast country, impossible to police correctly, and covered by vast woodland and swamp in which it was possible to hide and exist. One wonders what made them do it, though it has been argued that they simply did not know about the Nazis' extermination policy.

I can't imagine any group of people in the British Isles behaving in like manner, so it has to be something to do with education and upbringing over a long period of time.

One other aspect of this is an ability to develop extremely good skills which enable you to survive in a hostile world. In fact you become valuable to the people who despise you, and continue to despise you even when taking advantage of what you have. One thinks of course of Shylock, which shows us much of what the Elizabethans thought, but we also have Disraeli – admired and despised in equal proportions – and the fact that it was Jewish money which enabled us to grab the shares in the Suez Canal when we were a bit short and needed the cash quickly (Rothschild).

Later, much Jewish money and other treasures went to the Nazi chiefs via the Swiss, who are somewhat loath to cough up stolen funds even now; and even in the prison camps, Jewish bricklayers, plumbers, and carpenters found it easier to stay out of the ovens if they worked hard, than intellectuals and writers did. Even the musicians gave concerts for the Gestapo, carefully playing Wagner of course (another prize Fascist).

One sees the eternal struggle in modern Israel, and one still sees remnants of the old submissive Jewish legacy, even when it is blindingly obvious that Arab leaders like Arafat have no time at all for any form of compromise, and simply want to get rid of the lot of them in one way or another.

Some of the younger Israelis seem to have got away from this aspect of their heritage and one can't help but admire their strength and determination, as well as the fact they have learned to hit back hard and rapidly. The downside is that if you are a persecuted people then you stick with your own, and distrust outsiders. This is why it is hard for Jews to tolerate mixed marriages, and why in business they are such difficult competitors. These again are factors which cause dislike, plus the fact that if they have money they enjoy showing it – with less reserve than the English, for example.

They are also generous with their own people, which is another aspect of survival. Everyone knows of the support Israel derives from the large Jewish–American community.

We sometimes forget that Christ was a Jew. It is no bad thing to remind ourselves of this very frequently, since one could argue that He left it to others, particularly Paul, to spread the Good News to the Gentiles. Christ was not a 'Christian' but a Jew, and I would suggest that a case could be made that the differences between Christian and Jew are much fewer than the similarities.

Likewise, there is a similar connection between Christian and Muslim, and between Muslim and Jew. We are all 'people of the Book', and we are all monotheistic. Compare such cases with the differences between a Christian and a Druid, or a Jedi Knight, or some fey mooncalf rattling her crystals and waiting for the cosmic vibes. The problem for Christian, Jew, and Muslim is that very often the minor differences factored in over time have long ago been puffed out of all proportion and remain sources of great conflict. (For instance, was Christ *the* Messiah question; the foreskin question; the burkha and headscarf question; the kosha food question; the alcohol question; the transubstantiation question etc. etc., ad infinitum et ad nauseam.)

One of the most engaging things about the Jews is that somehow they have seen the fundamental idiocy of this aspect of human life and have developed the most engaging, sardonic, and magnificent sense of humour. They don't crack jokes so much as commentate on the ultimate anarchy of much of what we experience. (Woody Allen. 'My wife once taught dyslexics. She had one kid so bad he could only spell his name correctly. Luckily it was Otto.' If you can not laugh at this, you simply have never engaged with the deeper side of life and its thoroughly black nature.)

So it was a strange week in which two themes dominated. Christ's simple message to believe in him throughout everything that happens did *not* get lost. But again sin, persecution and death, the evil nature of bigoted, paranoid 'leaders', and their sycophantic followers, and the strange twisted fate of a complex people alternately loved and tormented by their God, and their convoluted attempts to cope, created a fascinating but unresolvable fog which did not exactly make it easy to reach any conclusions as to how the two themes were related.

I remain just as puzzled now as when I began, but I think I realise there are no easy answers. I just hope that suffering is not an obligatory part of faith for a Christian, as it appears to be for a Jew! Unfortunately, Ignatius and his exercises appear to have been heavily influenced by this and there seems to be a certain tendency to suggest that it should at least be a voluntary part, i.e. if you aren't sinning and suffering too much, then for Heaven's sake simulate it! (Or have I got it wrong?)

My point is that of course an understanding of pain and suffering is crucial to our development as human beings, and that without this we can not even remotely begin to understand Christ. But enough pain and suffering will find us easily enough. Perhaps too much. It is at such times we should reflect on Christ's suffering, though understandably we concentrate far more on trying to remove the causes of what we are enduring. If we did use such times to reflect a little on what Christ endured for us, I think it would be wiser and more effective than trying to imagine or simulate pain and suffering with the same end in view.

Reflections… January 30th

After the complexity of last week, and the plethora of information concerning the history and the culture of the Jews, this week has by contrast been like trying to grip smoke.

We are asked to be with Jesus as He leaves home to start His short ministry with His own baptism by John in the river Jordan. A moment's contemplation of the effect of that short ministry and its enduring effects over the last two thousand years leaves us amazed and slightly breathless at its power.

By contrast, studying the Nazi 'ministry' which took very much longer, involved vast expenditure, employed hundreds of thousands of people, and disturbed the lives of millions more, one is hard put to find one lasting effect barely half a century since it finished. One is therefore faced with the question as to what exactly it was which gave Jesus the power to have such an effect. A modern psychologist contemplating most human abilities is very loath to ascribe the development of any capacity to either genetic inheritance (nature) or upbringing and environment (nurture.) Most hedge their bets by saying most capacities are the result of a nature/nurture interaction, which usually leads to a rather fruitless argument about percentages, e.g., is intelligent behaviour the result of 60% nature and 40% nurture, or vice-versa?

When we look at Christ's ministry it would be simple to ascribe its effect solely to the fact that Jesus was the only Son of God, and therefore God (nature in this case) is completely responsible. I can see the power and attraction of the argument, in fact accepting it gets rid of a lot of awkward questions. But if it *is* the case, then one is rather puzzled why God bothered to ensure that Jesus was born as He was, in the situation that He was, with the chosen parents that He was given.

It is always stressed that 'Christ humbled Himself to share in our humanity', and there is no doubt that Mary and Joseph were ordinary people. Nazareth and Galilee were not exactly the swinging metropolis of the time, either, and to the grandees of Jerusalem Christ must have appeared as another troublesome 'hick from the sticks'. It seems hard to escape the conclusion that God was perfectly well aware of the effect of nurture on nature long before any psychologist, and one can only speculate on His reasons. Certainly, human beings have a greater tendency to listen to people trying to influence them who have shared their own experiences, rather than someone who has not. 'You don't know what you are talking about!' is always the immediate response when we sense that this shared experience is missing or is being hypothesised about. So it would have done Christ no harm at all to have been recognised as someone who had gone through exactly the same life history as His audience.

But God sent His Son to be born and to grow among human beings, and it is a bit too much to believe that He sent His Son 'pre-packaged', as it were, with all His teaching locked into His brain in some adult form, waiting until He was thirty years old or so, and could then use it.

It must have been there all right, but more in the form of a seed or a capacity which depended on – in fact totally needed – the human environment to bring it to fruition. We know when Jesus was twelve or so, that Joseph and Mary 'lost' Him, and discovered Him three days later in the Temple arguing with the priests, which is very much a case of nurture bringing out the talent. Certainly, the priests appear to have recognised the existence of the talent at that early stage.

This is why it is annoying, bewildering, frustrating, sad, infuriating, and lots of other frustrations as well, that we know so little about the further upbringing of Christ. He seems to leap onto the world stage in His early thirties, does amazing things in such a short time, and then like a meteor is gone from human sight. What on earth – literally! – did He do between the ages of twelve and thirty? What role did His parents play in this period? Who else might have had an influence on Him? What did He Himself do, either alone or with God His Father to prepare for His mission?

As I said at the start, this is where it is like gripping smoke. We can only speculate, and most of that will be done from the standpoint of our own experience. We can well imagine that His adolescence would continue the trend seen at twelve, that He would be totally concerned 'with His Father's business'. We can imagine Mary and Joseph not fully understanding this, but Mary influencing Joseph to stand back and let it happen, since she was more privy to what was going on.

We can imagine that the synagogue and the priests would continue to figure largely in His life. We can imagine that prayer, studying the scrolls, and long periods of solitude would play a part also. But we can imagine too that normal life would still play a large part in His experience, since His use of parable and image in His Ministry shows how wide-ranging this must have been. But whether Jesus left home at eighteen or thereabouts, or stayed at home until He was baptised, we have absolutely no idea.

I am inclined to think He left home early on. He makes frequent references to how necessary it is to give up everything, including family ties, if one wishes to follow Him, and on one occasion is certainly cool when told members of His family are outside waiting to see Him. So perhaps the long period of His twenties was spent simply preparing at length for his Ministry in all sorts of ways, giving nurture the final chance to bring out all that was given to Him by God. We see this process in other human beings who often serve long apprenticeships before being called to a position of great responsibility, Winston Churchill being as good an example as any. Certainly, Jesus' time was not wasted, for at His baptism we hear God saying, 'This is my beloved Son, with whom I am well pleased.'

For Joseph and Mary, in reality I suppose more 'foster' parents than we realise, it must have been very hard to see Him leave, and they must have suffered. We hear little more of Joseph, but we know Mary was present at His crucifixion, and we can guess at a little of the agony she endured. She is rightly venerated, and it is totally understandable that her help is daily sought by other mothers whose sons leave home for dangerous places or in uncertain times. We can be equally sure that she and Joseph provided optimal nurture for Christ both as child, adolescent, and adult until He felt that their task was completed, just as God knew they would.

One final thought occurred to me, which was that perhaps the total lack of knowledge concerning the formative years of Jesus is not an accident or unfortunate omission. Perhaps it is just our twentieth century 'nosiness' in wanting to know all the details that makes it seem so. They are after all of no real importance. What we have got is what we really need, that is Christ's teaching.

How it formed, where, when and why is really an irrelevance. The glory is that we have it, and that is what we should concentrate upon, which when you think about it is the point that lies behind a lot of Christ's remarks concerning friends, possessions and families, including His own.

There is only one true commitment for anybody in His view…to God the Father.

There's the crux, and there's the problem. For most of us family is very important. Most parents do not relish their children leaving home, unless something very unfortunate has happened in the relationships. Children find it hard to be separated from home also. It takes quite a time for the teaching of Christ to sink in, that we are part of a much larger family sharing the same Father, and destined to be all together with Him in Heaven for eternity.

It also takes some believing!

Reflections... February 6th

I always have had trouble with the phrase in the Lord's Prayer, 'Lead us not into temptation.'

I've almost never been able to say it or think it, without the question coming into my mind, 'Why would a loving God *want* to lead us poor sinners into temptation in the first place? Surely that is a very bizarre thing to do? He must know we have enough trouble avoiding it anyway without gratuitously wanting to add to it?'

For some years now I've altered it just for myself into '...and let us not fall into temptation,' – which seems to me a quite understandable request to make to God, and removes Him from being the likely cause, if somehow I find myself knee-deep in trouble after yielding to some temptation or other.

This view has changed markedly this week, as a result of being asked to think about the temptations of Jesus following His baptism, and coming across the writings of John Drane in connection with this (*Introducing the New Testament*, John Drane, Lion Publishing).

Both Luke and Matthew give us accounts of the temptations of Jesus. In Matthew, Jesus is asked to turn stones into loaves; throw Himself off the parapet of the Temple in Jerusalem; and is offered the world and its wealth in return for worshipping the devil. In Luke, the temptations are the same but the order is not. There we have the stones into loaves; the offer of the world; and then the invitation to throw Himself from the roof of the Temple.

Interestingly, the recorded responses made by Jesus differ very little. To the stones into bread temptation Matthew records Jesus as saying,

'Man does not live on bread alone, but on every word that comes from the mouth of God.'

While Luke records Him as saying,

'Scripture says: "Man does not live on bread alone."'

To the Temple temptation we have Matthew with, 'Scripture also says: "You must not put the Lord your God to the test."'

And Luke with, 'It has been said: "You must not put the Lord your God to the test."'

To the offer of the world, Matthew records Jesus replying, 'Be off, Satan! For scripture says: "You must worship the Lord your God, and serve Him alone."'

Luke's version is, But Jesus answered him, 'Scripture says: "You must worship the Lord your God, and serve Him alone."'

The meaning in every case is pretty clear, though Matthew's longer recorded response in the case of the stones into bread I think is the clearer one. As a child listening to Luke's version there was always the temptation to add, 'True! You need a bit of meat, fruit and vegetables for a balanced diet' – a response not guaranteed to earn many brownie points from the vicar on those long punitive Sunday school afternoons. But until I read Drane I do not think I had understood the deeper significance of what was going on in these temptations.

According to Drane, one has to see them as a crucial part of Jesus' baptism; in other words neither the baptism nor the temptations can be fully understood if studied independently.

Last week I speculated on how Jesus had spent His adolescence and twenties in gaining experiences to help in His ministry.

I had far too easily assumed that He knew perfectly well what that ministry would entail, even though I had postulated a nature/nurture process in getting there. It had not occurred to me that even while being baptised He might not be too sure what exactly it was He was going to be called upon to do. Drane says,

> According to Mark, Jesus heard the words 'You are my own dear Son. I am pleased with you.'
>
> This is a combination of statements found in two passages in the Old Testament. On the one hand there is an echo of Psalm 2:7;
>
> 'You are my Son, today I have become your Father.'
>
> In its original context, this statement referred to the kings of

ancient Judah. By the time of Jesus it was widely regarded as a prediction of the coming of the Messiah. On the other hand there is also a clear allusion to the poem of the suffering servant in Isaiah, where the servant is described as 'the one I have chosen with whom I am pleased.'

This idea of the servant was never connected with the expectation of a Messiah before the time of Jesus. It therefore seems likely that at His baptism Jesus learned two lessons:

He was reassured of His own special relationship with God as the person who had been specially chosen to inaugurate God's new society; and He was also reminded that to be God's promised deliverer meant something very different from what most people expected. It meant the acceptance of suffering and service as an essential part of His life. This was very difficult as Jesus was soon to discover. But He faced the problem with the power of God himself - something of which He was reminded when the Holy Spirit symbolically came to Him in the form of a dove.

Immediately following His baptism, according to Matthew, Mark and Luke, Jesus went out into the desert for the 'forty days and forty nights', fasted apparently during that time, and was tempted by Satan or the devil.

I think we can forget the forty days and nights as a true record of the time spent, plus the fasting for that length of time, plus the gentleman with the forked tail and horns. Much more likely was a lengthy hungry period, spent alone, wrestling with the sudden appalling realisation of what His mission and ministry truly entailed. (It must have been a truly gut-wrenching time, a precursor of the even worse time He would have in Gethsemane, when surely with this hindsight He told His disciples, 'Pray not to be put to the test.')

At such times you do not need a devil or Satan. Your own 'inner demons' of fear, terror, cowardice and self-preservation will all do nicely.

According to Drane,

Jesus was challenged to get his priorities right as God's promised deliverer, the Messiah. Each of the temptations He faced was a temptation to be that deliverer in a way which would NOT involve the suffering and humble service that Jesus now knew to be God's will.

Armed with the power of God, Jesus might well have taken the role of an 'economic miracle-worker' (turning stones into bread) and concentrated on giving the Jews the material prosperity so often pictured in the Old Testament as part of the New Society they were awaiting, when the hungry would be fed and all material needs satisfied. But He well knew that there can still be a terrible spiritual emptiness even when this is the case (one only has to look around now!) and that there are deeper needs satisfied only by 'every word from the mouth of God'.

He also might have leapt uninjured from the Temple top, and so given the credulous a 'Sign' that He was indeed the chosen Messiah. According to Paul the Jews demanded such Signs, and the habit has by no means died out among sophisticated Gentiles either. This would surely have put God to the test to save Him, but as Jesus by now well knew, this was not the way God wanted Him to proceed: it was likely to be a misuse of divine power for selfish ends, i.e. getting Him out of doing what God truly wanted Him to do.

We know He performed miracles later using the power, but they were always in support of His mission and never ends in themselves. In fact we know He very often pleaded with recipients to keep very quiet about what had happened. (They could not of course.)

He could finally have been the political Messiah, which is precisely what the Jews wanted the Messiah to be (which is probably why Matthew puts it last to emphasise its importance.) How tempting it must have been to have seen Himself kicking the Romans out and inaugurating the New World Order with Himself in charge.

Even now we have a seemingly endless succession of fools who keep trying to do it, and an even larger collection of fools spluttering and fussing when we finally gird up what is left of our moral courage and boot another megalomaniac swine into obscurity. No World Order ever succeeds when imposed from outside, and as Drane remarks;

...and Jesus saw only too well that what men needed was to give their will and free obedience to God, so as to be given the moral freedom to create the kind of new society that God wanted them to have.

Ruminating and reflecting on all of this has been a considerable learning experience for me. I'd totally underestimated the temptations Jesus was up against, totally and completely got too slight a grip on it all.

Moreover, I had slipped into the old Christian tradition of seeing 'temptation' as something to do with sex, or drink or something equally venial.

What Jesus was up against, was seeing with a sudden awful clarity that the mission which lay ahead of Him and initially might even have flattered Him, was in fact a truly awful Via Dolorosa with an unavoidable and appalling end, and yet even while the full horror sank in, lying to His hand was the unimaginable Power of God, which if misapplied would get Him out of it.

Even now, I am not sure I, or anyone else for that matter, can truly be with Jesus in that situation. I can't imagine the depths of His feelings as He contemplated His future. As He shared in our humanity, He *must* have had some doubts as to whether God would truly save Him – because we do.

Yet alone, hungry, tired, totally shattered and (I would have thought) devastated psychologically, in every case He rejected the temptation. No wonder He later told his disciples, 'Pray not to be put to the test.'

He knew them very well by this time, and knew it was beyond them to resist, as it was with Peter.

It's beyond me as well. I know there are some versions of the Lord's Prayer which include phrases like 'and put us not to the test' as a substitute for 'and lead us not into temptation'. I have never liked them because I did not fully understand them.

I still don't like them but I understand them better now. I think I will go back to saying 'and lead us not to temptation, Lord', because if He ever puts me in a temptation situation calling for the reserves of will power that Jesus showed in the face of such a challenge, I do not have a cat in hell's chance of measuring up. I would be reaching for whatever way out there was, and justifying it better than any politician, despite the sterling examples we are currently watching. But I am so very, very glad that Christ my Saviour did not.

Reflections… February 22nd

It's been a bit of a hotchpotch fortnight really. I've done rather a lot of reading, which I think has been the stimulus for a lot of disparate thoughts, and I've perhaps spent too much time trying to tie them together, rather than stay fixated on the Two-Values System. I have to confess to a fair degree of irritation also. This began when I ploughed my way through Fleming, pp. 136–148. I get twitchy when I read about Lucifer, since it seems to me that Fleming regards this 'false angel of light' as having real bodily substance; and for the life of me, I can't. Evil exists, undoubtedly, but the idea that there is some cosmic struggle going on between the forces of God on the one hand, and the forces of Lucifer on the other, is a bit too medieval for me.

Its roots lie in Zoroastrianism, which is based on such a struggle between the good God, Ahura Mazda, and the Daevas, or evil ones. At the end of time Ahura Mazda will triumph, but until then he 'wins some and loses some', which allows Zoroastrians to readily accept evil in the world, while we poor Christians, Jews, and Muslims twist ourselves into knots trying to explain why a loving God permits evil to exist.

Fleming seems to occupy some uncomfortable halfway house, admitting the existence of a evil Daeva (Lucifer) and suggesting that we should all go for: '…spiritual poverty, and should it please God, and should God draw them to want to choose it, even to a life of actual poverty. Being poor, they will then find themselves accepting and even desiring the insults and the contempt of the world.'

> They will come to live a life of true humility. Jesus' strategy is simple too, although at first it seems a paradox. If I have been graced with the gift of poverty ('he emptied himself, becoming human',) then I am rich; if I have nothing of myself ('everything I have is from the Father',) I have no power and I am despised and

receive the contempt of the world ('even to death, death on a cross'); if I have nothing, my only possession is Christ ('Christ is God's') and this is to be really true to myself – the humility of a person whose whole reality and value is being created and redeemed in Christ. Through these three steps, Jesus and his apostles lead people to all other virtues.

This makes me even more twitchy. I have to agree that as a system for dealing with evil it would work, but only if *everybody* followed it and that means Hitler, Stalin, Mugabe, Saddam, Bush, Blair and every jumped-up tinpot little dictator occupying every position of authority one can possibly imagine. What realistically is the chance of that?

Zero, nada, zilch – obviously – and I suspect Fleming knows it, which is why he goes immediately into raving masochist mode 'accepting and even desiring the insults and the contempt of the world'. Reading between the lines I suspect that his message is for the people who also really see no hope in defeating evil, or even combating it, so the best hope is to become so self-denigrating, abject and poor, that to all intents and purposes you give up on this life, but you give yourself a good chance of getting to the head of the queue for the next one.

I've probably been grossly unfair to Fleming, but there's something almost creepy about his obsession with sin and self-denigration which puts years on me. Why go actually looking for it? God knows it finds you readily enough!

There's got to be a better middle ground, certainly one which is more optimistic about this world and life. More 'God for England, Harry and St George!' An attitude, surely, which is not so wimpish, and appeals to the fighter in one. Following this line of thought led me to the problem of evil. By one of those happy coincidences I had just purchased Nigel Warburton's book, *Philosophy: the Basics*, which has an excellent chapter on the problem of evil. He poses the problem which is that evil exists, both man-made and natural. Why therefore does an all-good, all-powerful God permit it to exist, since if He is all-good He would not want it to, and if He is all-powerful He can stop it. Warburton reviews three solutions put forward by Theists:

1. Although evil in the world is not a good thing, it is justified because it leads to greater moral goodness. Without poverty and disease Mother Theresa's great moral goodness would not have been possible. Without war, torture and genocide, there would be no need for heroes, saints, and great moral crusaders. The argument is basically rubbish because the amount of suffering (much often unseen and unrecorded) is far too great to justify any number of saints and heroes, and a world without pain and suffering is infinitely preferable to one stuffed with saints and moral crusaders anyway.

2. Some have claimed that the world needs evil as well as good for some kind of balance or cosmic/artistic harmony. Since the only person capable of seeing such cosmic harmony is God, then it looks like He permits evil so He can enjoy the total effect. This doesn't strike a soldier hanging on the barbed wire with his leg off as a particularly good idea, and it negates totally the idea of a benevolent God. In fact the conclusion would have to be that God is some kind of sadist.

3. The most important defence is of course the free will defence. The idea is that God has given every human free will, that is the ability to choose for themselves what to do. If we did not have it we would be simply robots, pre-programmed only to do good things. But since we have it, we have the choice to do evil if we wish. It is only because we have such a choice that moral goodness exists at all, because if we were pre-programmed for good only, morality is immediately redundant. Behind the defence is the unspoken premise that a world where free will exists must be a better one than one where it does not.

Well now, let's consider the objections to this very prevalent idea. Firstly, I suspect that a lot of people would prefer to be pre-programmed to do only good, if it got rid of most of the evil they face every day. Secondly, free will itself might be a bit of illusion, not only in repressive regimes like Mugabe's, but in democratic societies also, since none of us knows how far our behaviour is genetically or experientially determined, and sadly politicians are forever seeking ways to force us to conform to something or other.

One could argue that if God is omnipotent He could have created a world in which there was both free will and no evil; or He could have given us the illusion that we had free will but programmed us so that in fact we never chose evil; or He could have devised our free will ability to always sieve out evil options a priori.

Defenders of the free will thesis would argue that all of these cases are not cases of genuine free will, and Warburton says that

> ...it should be pointed out in the Free Will Defence's favour that most philosophers believe that human beings do have free will in some sense, and that free will is generally considered essential to being human.

Accepting the existence of free will, and it looks like we have to, leads to some further awkward problems. Belief in God involves believing in the fact that He sometimes chooses to intervene in human affairs in the form of miracles. If He does, doesn't that in some way qualify free will? If He does it in small things (like water into wine), why doesn't He in large things like stopping the spread of AIDS? Also, if He is omnipotent and created all things, why did He set up the laws and processes of Nature to permit sudden and appalling disasters, which certainly qualify as natural evil?

Or is He bound by them also?

There are obviously enough problems with free will and the forces of evil to keep us occupied for a very long time, and as I said, trying to reconcile them is almost impossible. In fact it *is* impossible, and one sees that human beings have long tried to set up some kind of foundation for dealing with them and going forward, which is what the Ignatian Exercises are in fact.

Warburton concludes:

> We have seen that there are serious criticisms which Theists need to meet if they are to maintain a belief in an omnipotent, omniscient, supremely benevolent God. One way of meeting many of these criticisms would be to revise the qualities usually

attributed to God: perhaps God is not entirely benevolent, or perhaps there are limits to his or her power, or to his or her knowledge. To do this would be to reject the traditional account of God. But for many people this would be a more acceptable solution than rejecting belief in God altogether.

Oddly enough, thinking about this provided me with that missing bit that I did not find reading Fleming. If we accept that God is not entirely omnipotent and can make the odd mistake (and given the size of the task He took on when He created the Universe and everything in it, that doesn't seem too outlandish an idea), then it behoves us as believers in Him to do everything we can to assist Him.

This means fighting evil in every form and in every way whenever we meet it, not whining how unworthy we all are and yelping '*Mea culpa!*' on every possible occasion (particularly when it's *not* our fault.)

I don't think Christ asked us to do that anyway. I think He asked us to help Him build His Father's Kingdom on earth, and He took away our sins to get rid of a heavy burden which would prevent us doing that. He wants workers not self-indulgent whiners. Ignatius' 'Two Values' are nothing extraordinary either. They simply point out how we impede ourselves in this task if we get distracted by riches, wealth, power, possessions etc. The three types of person concept is simply another aspect of this, since the first and second types of person are obviously influenced by possessions or status, and the third type of person isn't.

I did not spend a lot of time analysing myself, since I did this earlier, and I do not think I have changed much. I know what the task is, and I am well aware of my failings and limitations. What was new this time was the feeling that maybe Warburton was on to something when he suggested God maybe needs our help much more than we realise in the fight against evil. It certainly gets rid of a lot of other very difficult problems if we too easily assume His omnipotence. Maybe those wily old Zoroastrians knew something after all…

Reflections…February 26th

This week has seemed a short week in some ways. It doesn't seem long ago that I was also sitting here contemplating my 'reflections' and wondering what I would end up writing, and whether it would accurately represent what I had been thinking about. Perhaps the long effort of the last fortnight tackling the great problem which confronts a Christian – that is, the problem of evil in the world – is still resonating.

This week's task does not seem to have quite the same gravitas somehow, though it is not without significance. I am asked to consider the three stages in the development of personal relationships. The first stage is a 'not-too-demanding' relationship, characterised by chatting impersonally and superficially, typified by a coffee morning or some such meeting. The second stage is typified by more regular meetings to share personal interests, helping out in a difficulty or crisis, but not sharing things at a deeply personal level. The third stage is a deep relationship, typified by complete mutual trust and the sharing of all thoughts and experiences, however personal, and characterised by empathy with the other. I am then asked to apply these stages to my relationship with God.

The first thought that occurred to me is that it is slightly faulty to do this without considering one important proviso. Man is by nature a social animal, and has always been so. We live and work in groups and societies of one sort or another – clans, tribes, friends, families, sisterhoods, brotherhoods, state and commercial organisations etc. – and very often we live in more than one group.

Life as a solitary, totally unattached individual is rightly regarded as a major handicap in life, likely to be the cause of all sorts of physical and psychological problems. The elderly are most likely to suffer this stage unless they live in a culture which does not permit it to happen, though increasingly in our capitalist world the young are beginning to suffer the phenomenon also. Living as we do in various groups it would be quite wrong to see the three stages as something we *must* go through in each and every one of our relationships. It would of course be lamentable *not* to reach it with my wife, and eventually my son. But it would be utterly absurd, and most likely impossible for me to try to reach stage three with my boss, my golfing friends, my lady friends, my accountant and my onion seller. I would not want to, and I am quite certain they would not wish it either. But there are others, of whom I am well aware, who would disagree with this viewpoint.

I remember being sent as a young lecturer by my Principal, to join a three-day Tavistock Clinic training course, only because she did not know what it was, and I was the cheapest way of finding out.

There were twenty people on the course and we were virtually locked into the training room for twelve hours a day, and had to sleep on campus also. The Tavistock Clinic then consisted of a rather unusual group of psychologists who regarded each person as being rather like an onion in that there were separate layers to his or her being, and that somehow the 'real person' was right in the heart of the onion.

Their training consisted of trying to peel away the layers of the onion, with a series of mystical exercises so that this 'real person' was revealed. It was almost an article of faith with them that we should all be better off if all our relationships were based on such inner 'real persons'.

I remember being totally horrified at being asked to pair off with a stranger and whisper in his ear the thing about my own personality of which I was most ashamed. While I was contemplating whether it was picking my nose, or a tendency to break wind quietly in public, the other guy rushed in to start to tell me some intimate details which affected his private life. Luckily a quick burst of, 'I don't wish to know that!' stopped him before it got too bad. I often think priests turn to whisky so frequently because of what they have to listen to in the confessional. I know I would.

I was glad to see I was not alone in objecting to what was being peddled.

The group of twenty on the intensive three-day course rapidly broke into two groups, who became known as the 'bleeding hearts' and 'the stiff upper lips' who ended the course disliking each other intensely, and the only woman present got savaged by both sides for trying to heal the breach. 'Why don't you sod off and look after your husband?' was about the nicest thing anyone said to her throughout.

The organiser from Tavistock mournfully and sorrowfully said it was the worst group he had ever had to deal with, and seemed to hold me and two others personally responsible. (I fell out with Tavistock again when another Principal brought them in to sort out management problems. I was asked this time to 'draw a critical incident' which badly affected the work of my Department. I said we didn't have any, but felt being asked to do things like this might qualify!)

The whole point about relationships is that as humans we have many, and it seems to me perfectly reasonable that they should co-exist with each other, even though they may all be operating at different levels. It is also perfectly reasonable that sometimes an individual relationship may move up a level, and it is also perfectly reasonable to assume that a relationship may move down a level. (This is frequently the case with relationships between the sexes.)

Having conceded this, it is, as I said earlier, quite something else to assume all our relationships *should* move up a level. I have many first-stage relationships with my golfing friends, with ex-colleagues, with my chimney sweep, window cleaner, coal man, and onion seller. I have many second-stage relationships with ex-colleagues, neighbours, old students, and decreasingly cousins as they die off. I have few third-stage relationships remaining, other than with my wife and son, since my oldest and dearest friends are all dead, and I did achieve this stage with at least two of them.

It does of course take time for a relationship to develop and perhaps change level, and I would have thought that frequency of contact is a key variable; though sharing some kind of trauma or other significant experience can hasten the process. Oddly enough, my relationship with my two lady cleaners, whom I see regularly every Thursday, and have done for two years or more, is changing from Level One to Two as both are experiencing very difficult problems, and I find we talk about them far more as time goes by.

Turning now to consider our relationship with God, we see that the provisos and qualifications we make concerning our human relationships do not apply.

A Christian's relationship with God is the most important relationship he or she has, transcending all others. This is not to say that it excludes all others. It simply takes priority over all others.

Because God is Father to all of us collectively, He is Father to each one of us individually, and it behoves each one of us to achieve the same level of relationship with Him, as we would hope to do with our earthly fathers, spouses and children.

The fact that many people do not achieve Level Three relationships with spouses and children is irrelevant. The simple fact of the matter is that they should.

I can easily see the analogy between the three levels that exist in our human relationships, and how these might be replicated in our relationship with God.

The 'Four-wheel' Christian has long been known in my church, i.e. he goes by car to church for his baptism, wedding and funeral, and not too many other times, and is not averse to saying the Lord's Prayer on solemn occasions, if he can remember it. The Level Two Christian I understand very well, as I was one for a very long time and probably still am. The Level Three Christian I can only aspire to, and I would not claim to be one yet.

But, I think I can say that part of the movement between levels in an upward direction certainly depends on knowing the nature of the higher level. As a Level Two Christian, I was unaware of the implications of moving to a higher level. It was relatively easy to attend church, to do a little charitable work, and to avoid the grosser non-Christian behaviours. Engaging in The Journey of Faith (which I did twice), and starting the Ignatian Exercises, alerts one to the nature of the task in moving up a level, and establishing a deeper relationship with God. It's a bit like setting out on a long journey. It's no bad idea to have an idea of where it is you want to get to, and it is no bad idea to have a map to help, both of which these exercises provide.

I suppose that was the idea behind studying the many examples this week of Jesus' encounter with various people. Each incident has its own message, of course, but I found myself looking for the commonality between them. What struck me was that no one was ruled out by Our Lord: no Roman, no Samaritan, no leper, no sinner, no child. They all received His undivided attention, His forgiveness, and what they asked. To receive this all He seemed to wish is that they made some small step or movement towards Him. 'Come unto Me, all you who travail and are heavy laden and I will refresh you.'

Just keep making a step in the right direction… Is that a bad idea to hang onto as we struggle to move up a level in our relationship with God?

Reflections... March 7th

I found this week's work just a little bit 'manufactured', which is perhaps the best word to describe those teaching situations which are slightly disjointed. As an ex-lecturer, I can remember hundreds of sessions, when after a fairly coherent input by myself, I was left wondering what I could then ask the students to do as a follow-up which would develop the work somewhat.

It was only after some long experience that I realised there was more to this than I realised. Very often the choice of student work could be very maladroit indeed, leaving the student totally nonplussed as to the relevance of what he or she was engaged in to the work that the lecturer had put in.

It was no good flannelling them that 'all would eventually become clear', as so often it never did, simply because it could not. Not enough thought had been given to the follow-up exercise. It remained a discrete entity in itself, what in the trade is called 'busy work'.

This feeling emerged as I read the instructions to this week's Ignatian Spiritual Exercise. The first part was clear enough which was to examine Jesus' reaction to 'unjust' situations, and those quoted were:

1. Jesus casting out the sellers from the Temple.
2. The parable of the rich man and Lazarus.
3. The woman taken in adultery.
4. Jesus refusing to be bound by hypocritical Sabbath day regulations.

The second part was to reconsider 'structural sin' and what I personally can do about it, in particular:

1. Probably I can fight injustice only in a small way, but am I doing something?
2. Our injustices to our planet, and so to future generations.
3. The parable of the rich man and Lazarus.
4. Am I becoming more aware of God's calls to me at this period of my life?

My first reaction on looking at the two lists was as explained in the first paragraph. There is of course much merit at looking at Jesus' behaviour in as many situations as possible, and in particular those where He gives some kind of explanation for what He did. Only then can we begin to understand the principles behind His behaviours and their relevance for us in our daily lives. (We have of course many of His teachings on what we *should* do, but only by examining what He actually did can we negate the temptation to level the charge that 'He says one thing, but does another' – which we all too frequently level at our other lords and masters, (e.g. the Minister thinks Comprehensive Schools are a good idea, but his/her children go to Eton).

But it did not strike me as *immediately* apparent, that an examination of Jesus' thinking and actions in the four situations quoted had much relevance for the four situations quoted in the second list. I could see vague connections, but that was about it, particularly as I contemplated soil pollution, dumping nuclear waste, and cutting down the rainforest.

This was when I started contemplating the problems of the writer, and feeling a vague empathy with another teacher in trouble grabbing at passing straws, and hoping things would be a bit better next session. But then a little humility kicked in, and I thought maybe I was missing something crucial, so I had better look a bit more closely at the quoted examples of what Jesus did.

His action in 'cleansing the Temple' is curious. Reading it cold and ignorantly, one gets the impression that the Holy Place, or even the Holy of Holies had been turned into a combination cambio and farmyard. In actual fact the money changers worked in the Court of the Gentiles, which was the only part of the 35–acre site where non-Jews were allowed, and this was a long way from the important parts of the Temple. One can appreciate His reason namely, 'Stop turning my Father's House into a market!' But it seems on closer examination to be a rather extreme action.

It is most unlikely that the money changers had moved anywhere else, since the way the Pharisees obeyed every other rule makes it most unlikely they would have been lax about this one. Also it was a bit rough on the sacrificial animal sellers, and particularly the pigeon sellers, who were there to provide the requisite sacrifice for the birth of a new child to people who could not afford anything else. Joseph and Mary had indeed used their services. So it looks like this was the action of a young man in a hurry right at the start of His mission, when perhaps maturity was in the process of forming. But one could not fault the principle, which was to acknowledge at all times the paramountcy of God, and the respect and worship due to Him.

The parable of Lazarus has I am sure brought comfort, throughout the ages, to millions of 'have-nots' who have been sustained by the thought that after a lousy time on earth, they will have a better time in Heaven. They have also drawn comfort from the thought that the rich are due to have a bad time, just to square things up. Jesus says elsewhere 'that it is easier for a camel to pass through the eye of a needle, than a rich man to enter the kingdom of Heaven'.

However, these days we are taught that this is not so, that God loves us all equally, so that if Hitler and Stalin will be there, we can expect to see Paul Getty, the Duke of Westminster and Bill Gates as well. I do not know what to think about this, particularly His final remark that the rich won't listen 'even if someone should rise from the dead'. Since Jesus knew He would do just that, He must have had a particularly pessimistic view of the impact of riches upon the capacity to develop a faith. But it is probably false to say all the rich are so tainted. Many are good Christians and give generously. Maybe He was suggesting that they have to be more aware of their charitable obligations than the rest of us?

The incident of the woman taken in adultery shows, I think, a much more mature Jesus, and a very skilful courtroom advocate.

The women was caught in flagrante, 'bang to rights' in modern idiom and under the existing Law was due for death. Jesus' act of twice writing in the dust is of course very mysterious, but is a wonderful way of spinning things out, particularly as He had just asked a very pertinent defence question, and suggested the first sinless prosecutor should throw the first stone.

This obviously gave time for thought, and caused those with something to hide to make themselves scarce, which eventually resulted in the woman getting away with it. One can imagine Jesus at the end of the incident drawing a relieved and very weary breath at the frailty of all humans, and then giving her a second chance out of bottomless compassion, and a deep understanding of temptation, and how easy it is for us all to sin.

The incidents on the Sabbath are the easiest to understand. Laws are for the containment of the stupid but the guidance of the wise, and should not always be seen as straitjackets. But this is a mature view, and also one which causes much trouble, for it causes people to have to think things out when laws conflict with wider moral issues.

We have plenty of current examples of that at the moment concerned with spying and eavesdropping and national security etc. It is very much easier to stick rigidly to the law under all circumstances and at all times. It removes the problem of having to think and also gives one a strong sense of moral rectitude. Extreme members of all faiths have a very regrettable tendency to do this, and it causes a vast number of the world's major problems.

Sadly, 'distorted faith' has probably killed more people in the course of human history than any other factor. God must indeed weep for us and our stupidity.

Turning now to 'structural sin', when I first studied it I concluded with a list of what I thought an ordinary person could do about it. (See 'Reflections' dated December 15th.)

Three months later, I see very little reason to change or amend any item on that list, other than to say I am even more convinced that writing letters or sending e-mails, and being aware of things happening that really do matter is of great importance. If only the millions who write, telephone, vote or scream about Big Brother would write, telephone, vote or scream about Darfur or Mugabe!

It remains to try to apply the conclusions drawn from the four examined incidents to the list. One can immediately see the implication for us 'rich' people in the West (and we certainly are by comparison), to help our Lazarine neighbours in the Third World, and those less well off here. We can see the dangers clearly of unbridled capitalism, and thinking about it shows us that we do not have to blindly accept the 'laws' of capitalism or the philosophy behind it touted by those it favours *particularly* by those it favours. We can object and refuse to follow them and indeed challenge them. Why should fat cat bosses get huge pay rises whether they succeed or not, or even if they do succeed? Likewise, when this week's 'offenders' are dragged into the public arena by the media and others, we can pause, doodle in the sand, and ask ourselves and others pertinent questions. Why not permit immigration if the immigrant wishes to work and contribute to our society, for example, rather than immediately pillory them as suggested by the *Daily Express*? If you want to clean the public toilets, then you cast the first stone might be a useful riposte. Finally, in all of these issues God remains paramount in the background. He watches us; He is asking, even demanding, we do His work. Anything which distracts from that, or moves too close and interferes with our relationship with Him, does indeed need driving out. So as an afterthought, apologies to my fellow teacher! He or she knew rather more about it all a priori than I did. I do see that the two exercises are connected, soil pollution and all.

Reflections… March 15th

It has been very hard to stay focused on this week's work. The task itself is clear enough, that is, to study various examples of Christ's teaching, and in particular to try to 'get closer' to Christ. I think I now have a better understanding of what that phrase might mean.

All too frequently in the past, I have read and listened to examples of Christ's work, and mentally thought, 'That's nice', or 'That shows deep compassion', or 'There's a message there for all of us'. But somehow it was all at a very surface level. My reaction was not much different to reading about the work of Mother Teresa, the Salvation Army, or a particularly nice troop of Boy Scouts in the daily press.

In other words it was all taking place at a distance, in time, in place, and most importantly at a psychological distance, i.e. it left me somehow untouched at a deep level.

What I think has slowly happened, and I'm not at all sure when the process began, is to see the work of Christ as much more personally relevant.

It's as if one is watching a well-loved teacher demonstrating and explaining something, and in a moment or two, one will have to show him that the point has been well taken, or the skill well learnt. In other words, the 'distance' effect has started to disappear, and it is as if Christ is here, now, and most importantly He is cutting down severely on my psychological detachment from Him.

I'm starting to feel guilty. It's not that I am feeling full of sin, and exuding all the foul miasmic sinful odours so beloved by Fleming. God forbid! It's just that I feel I am not quite pulling my weight somehow. I'm not fully part of Christ's team, and I am not at all sure what to do about it.

Then too, in more pessimistic moments, I have had to cope with an unwanted reaction which comes thudding back, possibly as a result of trying to cope with this new unease, when I find myself wondering yet again if we have got this business of faith all wrong.

Christ, however gifted, might simply have been one of those above-average good guys who periodically come along; did His very best in His time and place; but in His case suffered from particular delusions, badly overplayed His hand and suffered grievously for it.

He certainly has secured a place in history, along with Mahomet, Socrates, Buddha, Confucius, Gandhi, and all the other good guys, but such is the evil nature of mankind that they are all on a beating to nothing when it comes to trying to get human beings to love and live in peace permanently with each other.

Our attachment to the idea of resurrection, life after death, the kingdom of Heaven is so much 'whistling in the dark', since we can't really face up to the fact that life on earth can be nasty, brutish and short, and a large slice of humankind is actually pretty bloody nasty. There's more than a grain of truth in Marx's famous dictum 'Religion is the opium of the people.'

These two opposing ideas have been very much in the front of my mind all through the week. It was pretty clear to me what started it also. Like millions of others, I found the events in Madrid utterly devastating, and watched in appalled and horrified fascination as events unfolded. All the conflicting emotions were torn out of one almost simultaneously. Empathy, and deep sympathy for the distraught relatives; a desire to get up and do something... anything to help; savage fury and rage against whoever had carried out the atrocity, and a desire for revenge; utter contempt for the thinking behind such actions as in any way likely to advance any political process, if in fact that was the reason for it; then admiration for the thousands of people who simply came out to be counted and to grieve, and to show their solidarity and determination not to let this sort of action destroy them; finally, even a better regard for the world leaders who managed to find the words we all need at such times.

Then things got really sombre when it appeared that this action was part of the current Muslim jihad, not part of the Basque 'struggle'.

This hurls you back to confront the fact that these utterly

barbaric events are carried out in the name of faith. One immediately realises of course that not all Muslims are murderous fanatics; that most simply want to live in peace and coexist with the rest of us – with people of every faith and those with none at all. But the fact remains that the extreme bigots, the truly insane end of the spectrum, have somehow converted a benign faith into a foul, corrupt, theological and philosophical monstrosity, which justifies random and indiscriminate slaughter and somehow endows the perpetrators with the same kind of Heavenly glory as all the Saints in Christendom.

One can see it; one listens in appalled fascination to the benighted fools who peddle it; and sadly, one of the effects is to make one wonder whether if this is what can happen with faith, perhaps one is much better off without it. Perhaps it's better to accept that we live in a violent world, populated by far too many dangerous people, and spend our time building our defences, or getting as far away from potential trouble as is possible…

Particularly worrying and frightening is the totally antiquated nature of the extreme version of Islam. It is bigoted, anti-feminine, anti-American, anti-democratic, totally priest-ridden (far worse than the Catholic Church); and watching its young acolytes learning the Koran by heart always reminds me of the Chinese students I saw in the Sixties studying the *Thoughts of Chairman Mao*. It is a culture light years away from the West, and Madrid, (as Barbara Amiel writes in the *Daily Telegraph*) 'is what happens when the worst minds of the dark ages confront modern times'. Osama bin Laden wrote in 2001 about the 'tragedy in Andalusia' and what he was referring to was the liberation of the Iberian Peninsula from the Moors in the Middle Ages.

Others want the 'humiliation of eighty years ago' – the break-up of the Ottoman Empire – reversed, and all the lands freed from 'the infidel'. What can you do with people who regard America as The Great Satan? As Amiel pungently remarks:

> …given their rather bloody interpretation of the command of the Koran to spread the word to all infidels, unless we pull ourselves together we shall find ourselves spread all over the streets and railway lines. Let's pray by all means and then pass the ammunition.

Well the Jews, as represented by the modern Israelis, realise what we are all up against better than anyone else, and remain utterly uncompromising in the way they deal with it. They are after all right at the sharp end, day after day, while mercifully we in Western Europe only have to cope with the odd annual atrocity – so far at least – and after the obligatory few minutes' silence and piling up the flowers, we can all go back to football, and 'I'm a total nonentity, get me out of here' on the television. (Thinking cynically about it, that's not a bad motto for travelling on the Underground these days!) But Madrid represents a stunning victory for the violent fringe of Islam, since they have brought down a government, and will have forced the withdrawal of Spanish troops from Iraq. They will now push on inevitably and assault the rest of us. It is a question of where, not when.

So, I must confess that it was very much in this unhappy and pessimistic frame of mind that I turned to the readings this week, and also to other examples of Christ's work. The first thing that struck me was that Christ's teaching is actually timeless. It is true that the events and examples and allusions all belong to a bygone agricultural and pastoral society, but the principles do not. There is never any real problem in transferring them to a modern industrial, commercial and global context. Secondly, there is a profound and welcome absence of anything approaching jihad, this disturbing and aggressive militant aspect of Islam. True, Christ wants to establish God's Kingdom on earth, and it is obvious that He believed the process had started with Him, but there is never a suggestion of rounding up the troops and beating the crap out of the Gentiles. He is not averse on occasions to suggesting unpleasant fates for various kinds of offenders, but these are always offenders against His two cardinal Commandments, not unoffending foreigners. I'll sidestep the question of miracles. I've read John Drane's long examination of the phenomenon of a miracle. He argues in conclusion:

> In the miracles, God was demonstrating his own power so that men and women would realise that his long awaited kingdom had arrived with the coming of Jesus... The purpose of the miracles can therefore be helpfully compared with the purpose of the parables. To those who are willing to trust God they are the

vehicle of revelation. But to those whose minds are closed, not even a miracle will bring the possibility of enlightenment.

Whether this is true or not does not really matter when one is considering the response of a Christian to the onset of perverted Islam. The issue is whether to demonstrate the kind of passive solidarity that the Madrileños showed this week, to follow Christ in 'turning the other cheek', to meet violence with prayer and increased vigilance, but not incensed reaction against innocent Muslims in their midst, and to continue slowly and painfully to work for the establishment of the Kingdom of God on earth; or to follow the Israelis who obviously believe in 'an eye for an eye, and a tooth for a tooth', and keep the ammunition coming.

I honestly don't know the answer, but what I do know is that either way an awful lot more innocent 'faithful' of all kinds are going to die, and God indeed weeps for us.

Reflections... March 20th

It could be the continuing poor weather, surely one of the bleakest springs for a long time, or it could still be the resonances from Madrid, but I found it hard to be optimistic again this week. It could also be endless bickering and arguing that bombards one, on every television station one turns to.

It's as if we live in a world of spluttering, indignant people, who take every conceivable opportunity to splutter and be indignant about something, and so demonstrate their incredible moral superiority over the rest of us. For the first time I am beginning to have some sympathy for the people who resolutely switch off any social, religious, political, or quasi-intellectual programme as a matter of course, and concentrate on total trivia, football, pop music, or fairy tales for retarded adults, which constitutes the bulk of our so-called television entertainment.

If after all, our beloved leaders, the great mass of the world's movers and shakers, seem totally incapable apparently of agreeing on any single course of action about anything, even terrorism, what on earth is the point of listening to their endless arguments? Far better to watch *Coronation Street*, get on with everyday living, try to stay out of trouble, and hope the next bomb doesn't find you! It's very difficult to counter this view by arguing that the price of freedom is eternal vigilance, or that this supine 'head in the sand' attitude is what true political realists have always wanted, so that they can lay the groundwork for the next big takeover before anyone notices. Giving the proles bread and circuses is a long-established tradition. I contrast this with the period I experienced as a boy during the war. Then there was appalling danger every moment particularly in the early years when we lost battle after battle, ship after ship, and I well remember my mother trying to comfort yet another customer coming into our small corner shop, whose son or husband had been killed. Yet there was a clear unity, a clear solidarity, and above all Churchill led us with speech after speech of unswerving defiance in the face of an obvious monumental evil power.

Everybody listened avidly to the radio and no one was unaware of what was happening at large, yet no media person would have dreamed of attacking the actions of the Government, and anyone undermining the collective effort received very short shrift in one way or another. Now what we have is a split and divided people, enormous tensions, an almost flat refusal by many people and large slices of the media to even admit there is any virtue left in tackling obvious evils, like despotic dictators, simply because they exist.

Mugabe will remain absolutely untouched because of this lack of moral fibre, and so will the other despot in North Korea, unless he is stupid enough to upset the Chinese. It's as if we have totally perverted making moral judgements. It is now almost *more* moral to leave evil alone, since you can justify it by 'not interfering', or 'leaving people to determine things themselves' or asking, 'What gives us the right?' etc. It seems to be almost obligatory to attack anything that the USA and UK Governments do, yet no one seems to see that this kind of 'holier than thou' posturing covers over a truly huge lack of moral fibre to confront major evil head-on. I won't go into the problem of minor aberrations. My own Church will still be worrying about the rights of gays and lesbians to 'marry' each other and adopt children while Westminster Abbey is converted into rubble or an Al-Qaeda mosque. There is a much more worrying factor at work than tangential trivia like 'gay rights'. Much of this kind of negative criticism is done by Western intellectuals who have benefited from the kind of education where training obliges one to consider all points of view, and all sides of an argument. An unspoken assumption, almost a premise, which arises from this, is that any conflict is a 'problem' which by definition must have a 'solution', the means to which end is always 'discussion and compromise'. (This is at the root of the idea that to be educated means not just having a superior training in something, but to travel with a different frame of mind altogether from those not so educated.)

But there is one big problem with this premise. This kind of thinking does not apply to largely tribal or peasant communities, and it does not apply to the largely illiterate and unread peoples of the world. They get what little education they have from their group, and it is often very narrow, very unbalanced, very bigoted and very powerful. Neither does it apply to those communities where 'education and learning' is interpreted as the handing down of unchallengeable dogma by the leaders or priests, which simply has to be absorbed and followed.

The sad fact is that a large amount of the current evil in the world is the result of two or more groups of people, with some or all of these characteristics, being in conflict with each other. In Ireland it is the Catholic Nationalists and the Loyalist Protestants. In the Middle East, Muslim versus Jew. In Kosovo, the Muslim Albanian peasant, and the Serb Orthodox peasant. In Central and South America it is usually a communist versus a fascist. In Africa it is usually tribal. With Al Qaeda it is Muslim fanaticism versus Western liberalism. (Even Bush believes in democracy.)

Whenever natural disasters strike this simply adds to the total of man-made evil. It seems to be the case that it is easier for nations to cooperate to ameliorate the effects of natural disasters than it is for them to ameliorate the effects of the other evils. I also think that they have slightly better success when the differences are purely political than when they are not. What sadly, stands out for me, is that the most intractable problems seem to be based upon differences of faith.

Contemplating this constantly is something I find very wearying and dispiriting. I have been thinking about it very much recently and as I have said on earlier occasions, sometimes there is an awful temptation to throw up the hands and say 'Stuff all faiths. Faith kills, has always killed, will always kill, and the most faithful kill most!'

No wonder poor bewildered, atheistic or agnostic soldiers, policemen and fireman wonder what particular hell they have got into, as they drag the bodies out of another blown-up mosque, church, hospital, train, school, hotel or United Nations Aid Agency.

It does not help to turn to psychology either. One famous psychologist (Hans Eysenck) remarks that people are irremedially different, will always be so, and that there is little anyone can do about it.

One thing perhaps we could do is reject the idea of seeing everything from an educated 'problem/solution' basis, and start seeing them as 'situations' which are possibly permanent.

It might be bleak, but it's honest. The problem is that it adds to the pessimism, and the educated will never do it, as it guts their whole raison d'être. Maybe, though, our own television-watching peasantry have intuitively got hold of the correct end of the stick…?

So, again I turned to the readings for the week, prayer, and generally looking for something – anything, in fact – to throw light on these problems and if possible to lift the general gloom and depression. Well, I dutifully read everything and thought about it, and certain thoughts have emerged, for what they are worth:

1. I was glad there was no heavy emphasis on 'personal sin' this week. I really think this gets overplayed in our faith, and having to contemplate it yet again would have reduced me to either impotent tears or furious anger. It appeals to masochists, but I'll bet my last dollar that Osama doesn't worry too much about it.

2. Systematic depression seems to be a very large factor in our faith. I suddenly remembered that it was Lent when we are more or less ordered to be depressed and gloomy as we contemplate what Christ was faced with. I know it is because we can enjoy Easter all the more. Oddly enough, I felt a mite more cheerful as I contemplated the misery of all my fellow Christians. Schadenfreude works, okay?

3. Christ Himself is very often depressed. I'm beginning to think that He might even be a classic 'depressive' in psychological terms. He is very often depressed at the failings of His disciples; He is very often depressed by what He is asked to do, as in the raising of Lazarus, where there are frequent references to Him groaning, being troubled and weeping. He weeps over Jerusalem. The more I thought about it, I could not remember a reference to Him being happy, or laughing, or

dancing. 'Jesus wept' – yes indeed, there are many references. But, 'Jesus laughed'?

However, given His profound knowledge of what was His task, and what would be His end, and as He contemplated the faults and weaknesses of mankind, and even the failures of those who followed Him and loved Him most, who could possibly blame Him? It's absolutely amazing that He saw anything in us at all, or that we were worth His effort. ('Come unto Me all you that labour, etc.')

4. The Psalms by contrast I found uplifting and optimistic. Psalm 27 is a veritable paean to the love, strength, and protection afforded by God. Psalm 55 proclaims a belief that God will sustain even when one suffers persecution.

So I found myself decidedly cheered by the Psalms, which showed a powerful belief in God, plus frequent references to being surrounded by enemies, yet a secure belief that with God essential victory was assured. But then I noticed that Christ too always assures us similarly, when we get behind the surface depression.

I found myself imagining Him saying to me, 'Look! Forget My depression. I'm depressed because I know what will happen to Me and I am human enough to have some fears about that. But the true cause of My depression is that people have lost the belief and confidence in God shown in the Psalms, and I'm having an awful struggle to get them to see it. Regain it and you will overcome evil, and save yourself in the process. The Kingdom is coming to Earth, and God's will is being done. I know because I've started it – but there is a very long way to go. So join Me!'

Well, that is the true message of Easter, when the obligatory depression is supposed to lift for a Christian, because Christ comes into the world again, and we gird up our loins for another round with evil in all its forms. I found myself thinking, at the end, that despite the state of the world, the schisms, the endless carping, the madmen of other faiths, the intransigence of fools and peasants, there are only two choices, really, and there only ever have been two. You can pack it all in and watch teletrash, or you can pick up your weary, depressed feet one more time and trudge off after our beloved weary, depressed but ever-loving Lord, who in His way stands there confronting evil with even greater rhetoric and defiance and steadfastness than Churchill did.

Takes one to know one, and we depressives need to stick together, particularly when the wild-eyed zealots are loose, and have every intention of destroying us. Where are my shoes?

Reflections... March 29th

I must confess that I contemplated this week's work in a spirit of deep gloom and pessimism. Would we never get away from sin and suffering, I thought, and contemplate something which would elevate the spirits and put a spring into our Christian step? Why could we not as Christians develop some of the fervour of Islam, even though we would absolutely – and rightly – cringe away from the wild end, with its terrifying mullahs crying how great and glorious it is to be a martyr, and what a wonderful thing it is to send the infidels to perdition.

I now read that for years an American called Steve Emerson tracked Islam fundamentalists all round the USA, and actually filmed them calling for jihad quite openly long before September 11th. When he tried to get air time, the Administration and the networks chickened out, cut his programmes to ribbons, and the moderate Muslims remained so moderate as to be invisible. Only the extremists attacked him, recognising a fellow militant, and therefore someone to take seriously. Rather the same thing is happening to Lord Carey, who at least has had the guts to point out that there is something seriously adrift with Islam at the moment, and is getting nicely pilloried for it by the usual bunch of suspects. At least he's made me think that my Church has got some other interests other than homosexuality (yawn, yawn,) though I note glumly that it takes an ex-archbishop to open up the issue – not the current incumbent, who seems remarkably preoccupied with *Footballers' Wives* on the television. In fact I commend his tactic of trying to get the great unthinking to pay attention by using their own icons, but the message that the programme reflects much of our current social and spiritual malaise will get lost. I saw the producer of the programme smugly defending it as 'true to life', and condescendingly remarking that it affected more people than went to church, the appalling inference of which quite escaped him.

On the other hand, when I opened up my Fleming and read and reread 190 to 199, my initial feelings of gloom and despondency deepened and were fully justified. Immediately Fleming was asking me to ask God for the gift of 'entering into sorrow and shame... because of my sins'. Not only this but I hadn't just got to 'stay with external sufferings, but enter into the loneliness, the interior pain of rejection and feeling hated, all the anguish within Jesus'.

Well, at the risk of being I'm not quite sure what, – arrogant, unfeeling, cowardly – my first reaction was to hurl the book at the wall and say, 'I've been there, matey, for ten long years I've been there, after my first marriage broke up, and the only gift I want is to get as far away from a repetition as possible!' This of course led to a maelstrom of thoughts, which roughly analysed out as follows:

1. Perhaps I had sinned in my first marriage. I thought it broke up because my first wife claimed I was 'too cautious'. Maybe I was too preoccupied with work or saving or something. After all, what is a marital sin? Anybody got a list?

2. Perhaps it is a sin to think you are relatively sin-free? Fleming eternally implies that you are crusted with it all the time, like a ship covered in barnacles. Maybe I am. This of course led to a feeling of guilt, which annoyed me, since I did not know whether it was justified or not.

3. Perhaps the problem lies more with Fleming I thought. After all, he is a Jesuit, and with their track record, it is not surprising that he does not always seem to be a happy lad. Anybody who takes a kindly view a bit of self-flagellation, as I noted some weeks ago, needs to watch out for masochistic tendencies, and might benefit from a bit of assertiveness training. He certainly needs to get out a bit more, and perhaps spend valuable time contemplating the challenge of a much less introspective, mournful, and guilt-laden faith which is sweeping in again from the east. (If he has any sense of history, he might note we have permanently lost Constantinople and Osama wants Spain back!)

4. The problem could be Ignatius. I read his text, which in all honesty is less grindingly self-condemnatory and self-reproachful than Fleming, while making many of the same points. But I could not help remembering that this was a man who had a very chequered past, and felt he had much to be guilty about.

5. One thing I was absolutely certain about: no way was Essex Man going to give up *Footballers' Wives* for a study of Ignatius and Fleming.

Coming out of this lot, I was absolutely unsure of where I was, where I wanted to be, what I wanted to do next. I had done all the week's readings, which were well known to me apart from the Psalm, and I was well and truly hung up on the negative aspects of Christianity, and why we seemed to wallow and absolutely revel in feelings of misery, sorrow, sin, anguish, guilt etc. I roundly cursed – no doubt unfairly, and certainly bigotedly, stupidly, and obscenely – all Jesuits, all right-wing Spanish and Irish Catholics and my own homosexually-obsessed Church and the pestiferous 'holier and guiltier than thou' fraternity who made life such a misery for us poor peasants simply trying to hack it and stay out of trouble.

Then turning away from it all I was rewarded in a totally unexpected fashion. My wife had bought for me Bill Bryson's *A Short History of Nearly Everything*. Opening it up, I was confronted with the following:

Welcome. And congratulations. I am delighted that you could make it.

I know. In fact I suspect it was a little tougher than you realise. To begin with, for you to be here now, trillions of drifting atoms had somehow to assemble in an intricate and curiously obliging manner to create you. It's an arrangement so specialised and particular that it has never been tried before, and will only exist this once. For the next many years (we hope) these tiny particles will uncomplainingly engage in all the billions of deft co-operative efforts needed to keep you intact and let you experience the supremely agreeable but generally under-appreciated state known as existence. Why atoms take this trouble is a bit of a puzzle. Being you is not a gratifying experience at the atomic level. For all their devoted attention, your atoms don't actually care about you – indeed don't even know you are there. They don't even know that *they* are there. (It's a slightly arresting notion that if you pick yourself apart with tweezers one atom at a time, you would produce a mound of fine atomic dust, none of which had ever been alive, but all of which had once been you.) Yet somehow for the period of your existence they will answer to a single rigid impulse: to keep you being you.

The bad news is that atoms are fickle and their time of devotion is fleeting – fleeting indeed. Even a long human life adds up to only about 650,000 hours. And when that modest milestone flashes into view, or at some other point thereabouts, for reasons unknown your atoms will close you down, then silently disassemble and go off to be other things.

And that's it for you.

Also not only have you been lucky enough to be attached since time immemorial to a favoured evolutionary line, but you have also been extremely – make that miraculously – fortunate in your personal ancestry. Consider the fact that for 3.8 billion years, a period of time older that the earth's mountains ands rivers and oceans, every one of your forbears on both sides has been attractive enough to find a mate, healthy enough to reproduce, and sufficiently blessed by fate and circumstances to live long enough to do so.

Not one of your pertinent ancestors was squashed, devoured, drowned, starved, stuck fast, untimely wounded or otherwise deflected from its life's quest of delivering a tiny charge of genetic material to the right partner at the right moment to perpetuate the only possible sequence of hereditary combinations that could result – eventually, astoundingly, and all too briefly – in you.

Well now, I thought, God truly works in mysterious ways. Here I was stuck in some Jesuitical morass, like thousands of good Christians before me, wondering whether there was any point to faith at all, when laid before me was the absolute miracle of my unique existence. The more I contemplated it, the more my spirits lifted. I found myself swamped by a tumult of thoughts which took some teasing out.

1. One can only stand amazed at the fine details of one's construction. It is *not* a matter of regret that our atoms will end

up in future as a leaf, or a worm, or as part of another person. I find it a cosmic wonder that I may have atoms in me that were once part of a Roman legionary, or a dinosaur, or a shark or a Balinese dancer. I find it marvellous that the planet, or the Solar System, is a vast bowl of atomic soup from which everything and everybody is constantly re-distilled and recreated.

2. This to me simply illuminates the glory and unparalleled genius of God the Creator. There is a majestic cosmic simplicity about His work, despite all the fine detail of the laws of chemistry, biology, and physics etc. The births and deaths of far stars create the heavier molecules, carbon, oxygen, hydrogen, nitrogen, a spot of calcium, a dash of sulphur a few trace elements needed to make life. It's a short and simple list. They drift into our Solar System and are trapped, and there's the soup. Yet despite this, as Bryson says, the fact that I am uniquely here now is to win something of a lottery. One wonders how many other potential humans lost the lottery and never existed because of pestilence, war, accident, or something else breaking the chain that Bryson postulates is needed. Talk about luck!

3. Then I contemplated Bryson's image that if we picked ourselves apart, atom by atom, we would end up as a mere pile of dust, no part of which had ever been alive. Yet we are wondrously alive. So we are obviously *more* than the sum of our parts. What else could that extra bit be but a soul put there by God to inhabit our portion of solar atoms, for as long as He sees fit, and for some purpose He has in mind for us? I think it was the sheer impossibility and pointlessness of our being *only* a pile of atoms, curiously and inexplicably sentient for such a short period, which cheered me up most. If you believe we are, then you are perhaps better off watching *Footballers' Wives*.

4. Then I contemplated the role of Christ in all of this. When God has created such a magnificent system, it makes sense that He also gave us free will to fully enjoy the fruits of it, especially as 650,000 hours soon goes and someone or something else might need the atoms. (I am still puzzled why

we are only allowed such a short time and I now see 'sin' as wasting any part of that time.)

It is not implausible that when Christ warns against sin He is also thinking about anything which detracts from our making best use of our short time here.

Why was the women taken in adultery wasting her time being adulterous, he seems to be thinking.

Why are all these scribes and Pharisees wasting their time and My time worrying about it? Why don't they all bugger off and do something more useful like irrigating the fields?

5. But of course, and far more importantly, He also gave us the incredible Good News that there is more in store for us than a mere 650,000 hours, and that somehow makes far more real sense to me now after reading Bryson.

I need that belief like I need oxygen, to make any sense at all of this atomic world. If 'sin' is important, it is only because it gets in the way of spending our time wisely here.

I can't believe many of us have a lot of it, and I can't believe that even if we have, it will prevent us entering Heaven.

6. I am sorry Christ suffered so much. I am even more sorry that a large part of His sorrow and suffering is down to the fact that we do not realise how lucky we are to be here at all, and that it behoves us to use the short time very wisely and well for all our sakes. I am sorry that many still find it hard to believe the Good News, and that even Christians are not immune from doubts. I freely admit, that some things have only just started to come into better focus for me.

7. I understand the totality of the Church's year, and I understand the need to study Christ's birth, teaching, passion, death and resurrection, the totality of which is paramount and the cornerstone of our faith. I fully appreciate and value that only by doing this for some considerable time and in some depth will one come to realise what Christ was trying to do, and how this reflected the will of God. But I do think the emphasis is sometimes wrong.

8. I think that the tendency to concentrate on sin and suffering to

the extent shown by Fleming and others is misplaced, and self-indulgent, and possibly obscures the truly optimistic nature of Christ's message.

When *Footballers' Wives* even attracts the notice of the Archbishop of Canterbury; when church attendance is falling catastrophically; when the Pope is ailing badly and cannot retire; and when Islam is resurgent, we need Christian leaders of strength, fortitude, punch and above all optimism.

That optimism has to shine forth each and every time they speak to us. You simply can not allow yourself the luxury of turning watery eyes to Heaven, flapping your limp compromising hands around dementedly, abasing yourself, and yelping 'Mea culpa!' or of distracting us with the problems of a few strident Canadian homosexuals; or of slipping on your old relativist overcoat and finally nailing your butt to the ecclesiastical fence. Isn't it very odd that the only two Christian leaders anywhere showing any of the characteristics needed for this are Bush and Paisley? 'No surrender' indeed! What dinosaurs! Let's have a sneer-along with the *Guardian* and *Independent*! But... maybe the wrong context in both cases, but the right concept?

Reflections… April 4th

This is about the twentieth time that I have sat down to write these 'reflections' and since this is approximately two-thirds of the way through this particular series of spiritual exercises, it appears to be a good time to take stock of what has been happening, or perhaps not happening. To be honest, I'm not sure why it seemed a 'good time' rather than any other time: it might have been that I simply could not bring myself to contemplate any more sin and suffering, even though it is the start of Holy Week, when it is particularly appropriate to do just that. Naturally I felt guilty about this, and it sparked off at least three trains of thought:

1. There is only so much contemplation of suffering that one can take before the well of compassion runs dry and you simply have to get away from it. This is probably no bad thing since eventually if you do not, then you start to damage yourself.

    Psychiatrists and counsellors are overwhelmed by people who no longer seem able to rise above dealing with the normal amount of suffering we have to endure as part of life. I can't help feeling that my parents' generation dealt with it better, though the larger and more cohesive family and kin groups they enjoyed – also as a normal part of life then – gave them a powerful form of defence to use. I well remember the large number of people who were immediately involved whenever there was a death in my family, for example. Suffering shared is suffering pared.

2. But, unlike my parents' generation, we are now totally bombarded on television with images of suffering. We turn on the TV news in the grim expectation of another atrocity, slaying, famine, accident, murder, abduction etc., and we are rarely disappointed. This maybe has the advantage of making us more aware of events, but it also has the effect of exhausting our natural compassion, and many people simply

no longer watch the news, since their attitude is that it makes them sad all the time, and they can't do much to help anyway.

My parents' generation were spared this blanket coverage of suffering for obvious reasons, and got their bad news in very much smaller doses, either from radio bulletins or from very truncated newspapers.

3. The final thought was that the right and proper contemplation of Our Lord's suffering at this time, was being made more difficult because of our being swamped by the suffering all around us. It certainly is for me, anyway. I'm not suggesting there was ever a golden time of peace when such contemplation could be undertaken as something very different and unusual to the normal run of things, but it does seem to me that we are living in 'an age of recorded and viewable suffering' absolutely unparalleled in history, and it must be having some sort of effect which is certainly detrimental in some way.

So, although I saw the logic of being asked to contemplate the suffering and death of Jesus at this time, I simply had to leave this to take place during the services in Holy Week. I felt absolutely destroyed by the suffering seen over the last few weeks everywhere, and I felt I did not have it in me to give whatever deep empathy was required for this task.

I shall no doubt find myself doing it during Holy Week, but it will be more a question of it stealing up on me, than me going looking for it. There's something weak and pathetic about that, but it is how I feel, and all I can do is apologise to God, and remind Him I am only human, and unlike Jesus there is a distinct limit to what I can endure.

So, with a sense of relief I have to say, I turned to a sort of self-appraisal of what the last twenty or so weeks have meant, or what I have learned from these exercises.

1. I suppose it is useful to try to express the kind of Christian I was before I started. I've always regarded myself as one of the infantry in the army of Christ, and not a very good soldier at that. In terms of an army on the march, you would not find

me up at the front with the crack regiments and the bemedalled staff officers. I'm right at the rear with the baggage train, shuffling along in the dust and debris left by everyone else, sweating, cursing and grumbling, but at least part of it.

2. This never worried me. It is not false humility either. I am very certain of that. I was very glad to be part of the army at all, and there is absolutely no doubt in my mind that I wanted to be part of the army. I really do want to believe in the Good News brought by Our Lord, because if there is no resurrection for us, no Heaven for us, no being reunited with those we have loved and cherished, then this world makes no sense at all, neither does existence have any real point. The whole thing becomes inexplicable, indefensible other than as a giant cosmic joke and not a very funny one, either.

3. The problem is coping with the awful and appalling thought that in fact this is just what existence is. This I suppose is the meaning of 'doubt', as a Christian understands it. I can see that studying the work of Our Lord more deeply, and indeed the notion of 'getting closer to Him' is certainly one way of dealing with the problem of doubt. If one is more and more convinced of the truth of what He says, by deeper and deeper study of His life and teaching, then doubt should begin to disappear.

    Conviction and doubt are inversely related.

4. I can not say that my doubt has disappeared yet. I'd be very surprised if it did. But neither has it increased. I can honestly say that my need to talk to God is now firm. I suppose I started talking to him seriously in the 1960s, when my first marriage disintegrated, but it was mainly to make inordinate demands on Him to do things, which with hindsight I see He quite rightly ignored, while quietly and subtly helping me in ways I simply did not appreciate or was even aware of at the time.

    Now it is different. I'm uneasy if I do not talk to Him before I sleep, or when I wake up in the early hours. In fact I can't actually do it. Sometimes it's just a formal prayer; sometimes a vote of thanks for the day; sometimes a more heartfelt acknowledgement of all the many blessings large and small given to me; sometimes a discussion; sometimes, and this is the most difficult, just trying to keep quiet and listen to Him. I seem to need God much more, and in many different ways. Maybe as family and friends inevitably die, you see God as the one solid dependable and everlasting friend left.

5. Teasing out the role of the programme in this change isn't easy. To start with, I have had some problems with Ignatius, and a great many more with Fleming. I can take Ignatius' more spartan and soldierly approach, than the rather creepy Jesuitical approach. Also I think both Ignatius and Fleming have far less 'doubt' than I have.

   In the case of Ignatius, this is perhaps an aspect of his times. In the case of Fleming, an aspect of his vocation. But they seem to come at things from the point of view of totally committed Christians, needing to know Jesus almost as well as one of the disciples. Back in the baggage train, I am a long way from that.

6. At least the programme has the enormous virtue of being structured and getting one to read and study readings from both Old and New Testaments. Moreover, the fact that the reading is never very copious helps. You do get time to think about the readings, and above all try to see the relevance to one's own everyday living. But the intention is also to get you to develop a 'deep-felt knowledge of the Lord made man for me that I might love Him more and follow Him more closely'.

7. I suppose it is when I ponder this that it is hard to assess what has been happening. I certainly have reached conclusions about Him that I have never reached before. I think He is a great 'leader' in a truly subversive way. I think He was given a task and a load to carry which no human being can possibly comprehend in all its aspects. I think that this depressed Him beyond our understanding, and our own failings contributed immeasurably to this. It is right that we should at appropriate times contemplate this – not in a spirit of 'didn't He suffer!'(à la Mel Gibson), but in a more clinical dispassionate way.

   Why was it necessary for Him to do this? What had

humans done to so offend God that He felt it necessary to put His Son through this? Are we still doing it? ('*Yes!*' is the obvious answer.) What and when are we ever going to stop it? How do we stop it?

8. I can contemplate suffering in this light, and part of the programme (the handouts) I think rightly gets us to focus on that. I have trouble though with contemplating suffering simply as suffering. That seems to me to be self-indulgent, morbid, and not very productive. The whole point of contemplating it, seems to me to be to identify the causes, and if possible remove them. This seems a more fruitful optimistic, muscular kind of Christianity, than one which seems to wallow in the appraisal of it simply for its own sake.

9. This leads me to consider sin. I've had a lot of trouble with this all through the programme, and again it's down to the Jesuits. I can quite appreciate that Ignatius felt a sort of personal revulsion against his early lifestyle and a desire to put things right if he could. I have no problem with this at all. I have less sympathy with Fleming's ideas that somehow we are all *so* sinful that we have contributed immeasurably to Christ's load.

What on earth is some poor harmless pensioner, trying to live his life as blamelessly as possible, trying not to disturb God or his neighbours as far as he knows, to make of this? The message seems to be: 'No matter how hard you try, you creaking old bastard, you are still a sinful swine, and Our Lord is suffering as a result!'

I find this hard to deal with, and I find it one of the less attractive aspects of both our faith and this programme. Either we have it wrong, or our normal behaviours are far more sinful than we realise, or we have given the Jesuits too much scope.

10. I think too that trying to get closer to Jesus has forced me to consider the relationship between God and Our Lord. I pray to God, there is no doubt about that.

I rarely pray directly to Jesus, though I do pray to Our Lady also. I know that Our Lord said that no one can come to God except through Him, but I have not too much idea about what that means. I hope it means absorbing the lessons of His teaching.

The idea of the Trinity, which I understand is a late theological introduction, is a great mystery to me. I see Jesus as God's Son, and I see Him teaching us particularly about our failings in God's eyes, and the way of remediation. I see His suffering and death as God's means of wiping the slate clean, and giving us all a clean start, probably for the last time.

11. I think I am fully aware of what I need to do to play my part. After all, Christ made it very clear to us in all sorts of ways. I hope I am trying to do my small bit. The constant harking on sin and suffering I do not find helpful, since they generate guilt, and guilt is not morally a good motivator. If I want any motivator at all for good works done, then a smile, a nod, a 'Thanks, friend,' will do nicely.

12. So in conclusion, where am I? Still in the baggage train, undoubtedly but marching along a bit more cheerfully. (Rather more worried now though about my generals, and wondering why they are not watching the encircling bad guys with the bombs, instead of worrying whether the adjutant should be allowed to sleep with the quartermaster, and whether they ought to get 'married'.)

I'm enjoying some aspects of the training, the readings, and some parts of the manual. I find some of the training staff acceptable and one in particular a bit weird. I like my personal tutor very much, wonder how she puts up with my ramblings, and yet manages to keep encouraging me forward.

13. So, using a forced geological analogy, although the programme is not causing observable and seismic shifts in my Faith, as far as I can tell; that is not to say that deep down considerable movement is not taking place in the liquid magma of my beliefs. Something is going on, and the old phrase 'God alone knows what it is' might be very apt.

14. One thing is for sure. When He is ready He will let me know what it is. Meanwhile I will keep marching, and keep a very watchful eye on those bad guys.

Reflections… April 8th

I sometimes wonder, as I sit here at the start of writing another one of these reflections, what I will be reading when I contemplate the finished document.

Their origins lie in very different processes. Initially, for example, I sat down very much in the mode of writing an academic essay. I checked the source material; sketched out the relationship of the ideas in the form of a flow chart; sorted out the beginning, middle and end; and finally wrote the reflection.

As the weeks went by, this process softened, maybe 'blurred' is a better word. The planning was still there, but it had become more a mental process only, roughly sketched out during the early hours, and resurrected when the time came to sit down at the computer. This process lasted for quite a lot of the reflections.

Lately, however, the process has changed again. I have several times sat down with only a few ideas and images in my head, not really knowing how they fitted together a priori, but content to try to work out the significance and relationships as I wrote.

This process has been some kind of creative process, rather akin to cooking. I have the ingredients before I start, but have very little idea of what the dish will look and taste like, until they have been mixed and cooked.

This time I have reached another stage. I don't even have a pre-prepared set of 'ingredients' to work with. That isn't to say I have totally taken the time off during the last fortnight. I attended two out of the four services of Holy Week; I continued to talk to God and pray one way or another; I read the bulk of the prescribed references and even branched out a little. (Never having read the full letter to the Ephesians before, I found myself interestedly completing this.) I even found myself in mild hot water with my wife on Easter Sunday morning, for remarking to the priest that I did 'fifty-one masses a year, and then managed to get to my own church once.'

I still feel that to most devout Catholics, ecumenism is a total dead duck, despite what they say. They will never see it as anything other than a bit of 'slumming' among the poor; something to be put right with Father as soon as possible. Even my wife, who is most open-minded, has a problem with the Eucharistic aspect of it. (Mind, when I read that *yet again* the pernicious homosexual wing of the Church of England have wheedled their man into the Deanery of St Albans, after failing to get him made a Bishop last year, despite all the opposition both here and around the world, I absolutely despair.

If ever a Church was totally out of touch with what really matters; was so arrogant as to force its unacceptable minority ideas down the throats of its flock, it is this one. It is time to reverse the parable; time for the sheep to leave the bulk of the shepherds who are dependable, and go off into the wilderness looking for the 'lost shepherds' who have gone astray. I can't blame anyone of another branch of Christianity for wanting to have nothing at all to do with us. It won't be long before we shall have the last few heterosexual itinerant Church of England vicars scurrying round holding illicit services in houses, and hiding in 'priest holes', fearing discovery by the dreaded GBAS (Gay Beadles and Sidesmen) secret police. Common sense tells me that I can not be the only old male member of the Church of England who would find it unacceptable, offensive and disturbing, when on my knees in church worrying about the proximity of my soul to Almighty God, to discover that I was being seriously distracted by worries about the proximity of my bottom to the vicar. Such old survival skills and attitudes, learned in all-boys' schools and National Service die hard. But I digress.)

I actually spoke to God about the feeling that this time nothing was really coming through to me to reflect upon. It was as if I had come up against some kind of wall or fence. I suggested that if He wasn't too busy, He might like to put something or other in my head. I got the feeling that He didn't think the time was quite right that night, so why didn't I just sit down with my back to the wall and relax, imagine I was in the sunshine like I was last summer at Anderida Roman fortress on the Kent marshes, and just enjoy 'being'.

He'd prefer me simply to pray for all the poor desperate souls who needed it, just for the time being. When I was writing He would help. So I did, here I am, and He is. I am remembering thoughts I had before Easter Sunday. I am remembering the fickleness of the crowds, who welcomed Christ as he rode into Jerusalem, and then preferred to save a murderer when given the choice. I am remembering the enmity of the Pharisees and priests, determined to crush this upstart before He became a real problem.

I am remembering poor Pilate, fundamentally a good man but unable to maintain a principled stand, crumbling before the demands of those he was supposed to rule, and fearful of the actions of his bosses back in Rome if the province suddenly erupted if he made a mistake.

I am remembering Peter, suddenly realising he too could be in very big trouble, and reneging on his vows when the pressure was on. I am watching the populace going about the business of preparing for the Passover meal, totally oblivious of three wretched scarecrows being hurried off to Golgotha by the guards, and shrugging their shoulders even if they noticed.

I am remembering a botched execution which extended the suffering, and the dawning compassion of one guard who handed up his sour wine. I am remembering the NCO who had a better insight into what he was witnessing than all his officers had.

I am seeing the poor family and friends gathered around suffering and mourning, almost self-destructively aware of the injustice, inhumanity, snobbery, hatred, vindictiveness, and bigotry which had led to this, and how little the population at large either knew or cared.

Then, very sombrely, I am remembering how nothing has really changed. I could without too much trouble recreate the scenario either in part or in total in any of the world's trouble spots today. Two thousand years ago it all happened, and yet it is as fresh now as it was then in all its aspects.

Except one. I am remembering church now on Easter Sunday morning.

I am sitting very much on the sidelines at the Catholic Church of the Holy Cross. I tend to sit at the back or at the side in any church, much to my wife's irritation. She likes to be up front, where she can see all that happens. I like to be at the back where I can watch. I am very aware that there is a difference between 'seeing' and 'watching', which is almost the difference between being a player and a spectator.

As an Anglican in a Catholic Mass, one can only ever be a guest 'watcher', but it is not an unrewarding occupation. One watches everything, and watching and thinking about it constitutes reflection.

What I watched on Sunday morning was firstly and simply ordinary people.

I became very aware of their 'ordinariness'. They were either very young, youthful, mature, elderly, or decidedly aged. They came in all combinations; alone, in pairs, family groups – and even larger groups, since three girls were to be baptised during the service. They had every kind of skin, complexion, clothes and appearance, and yet no one really stood out There was no one who could possibly be described as a 'celebrity'. (Perhaps celebrities don't stand out in church either, only in people's minds?)

The whole scene reminded me of a Breughel painting, and some faces were indeed those you see in a medieval painting. Then I noticed there were no sad or angry faces.

There were wrinkled faces, lined faces, calm faces, still faces, smiling faces, but there were no faces twisted in agony or rage, or tormented by grief such as we see nightly on television after yet another atrocity.

Yet the faces all had something of the same about them. Reflecting further, I noticed the atmosphere had something as well. There was buzz and bustle; there was a lightness in the air. Hunting for words, I came up with *anticipation*.

As the Mass started and progressed this atmosphere did not go away, either. Yet the Mass was not really very different from the ones we normally attend. The baptisms were applauded, and the Easter eggs distributed to the children, but neither I felt could be held to account totally for the sense of lightness and the buzz which was still there at the end.

I was not immune myself to this feeling, and my thoughts went back a long time ago to an Easter Service in Bellagio on Lake

Como, when a very large and very volatile Italian priest stood on the chancel steps and exhorted his flock to *Gioia*! in stentorian tones. You didn't need too much Italian to know what he was on about.

And there it was: the missing element. The Good News. The amazing combination of joy, hope, anticipation, bustle and buzz which comes into the world anew on every Easter Sunday morning. That's what we were all feeling, even if we could not articulate it, and it would take many different forms.

To the old and tired, it was perhaps the welcome reminder that Christ had not forgotten them and never would, and had indeed made a place for them in His Father's house; to the baptismal parents it was time for the promises and determination to make sure the children would fully understand this most marvellous and true teaching; to the children that here was something of great importance, though as yet not fully grasped.

To the rest of us it was a time to move on from suffering, misery, death and destruction, to resurrection, new life, joy and hope.

I felt very sorry for that grieving group around the cross two thousand years ago. They only saw then what we see daily on our screens. In fact, we probably see much more of mankind's appalling negativity than they did; but they were yet to see and understand the miracle of the resurrection of Christ, and the amazing counterweight it brings against this negativity. We have had two millennia to see it, to understand it, to absorb it, and to rely on it.

But not all of us do, of course. I was glad to meet my old tutor Doubting Thomas again, in the readings. Of all the disciples, I feel I know him best of all. A nervous introvert is Thomas; it takes one to know one.

He needed proof positive, got it, plus a merited reproof, but he knew what he saw, did Thomas. His conversion was immediate and total and probably unbreakable.

But Christ knew we could not all possibly see the evidence at first hand, either then or now – hence His approval for those who could believe without having seen the evidence for themselves.

I do not think He or His Father set out to make things deliberately difficult for us, by making Faith some kind of metaphysical test to sort out the sheep from the goats. He knew that to extend His message would call for teachers of a very high calibre, hence His endorsement of Peter, and His later recruitment of Paul.

Neither let Him down again; but it also put a very large responsibility on all of us to take part in this teaching, actively and reflectively.

Both demand commitment, and that isn't easy. I found myself finally reflecting on the degree of commitment required. To a 'professional' Christian – and by that I mean priests, ministers, monks, brothers, sisters – such commitment is and must be total. It is and must be rooted in a call or compulsion from God.

This drive or call in many ways excuses the demands made by Ignatius and Fleming on us to share as deeply as we can in all aspects of Christ's life, particularly the suffering. After all, if nothing else at all matters to you in life but your proximity to Christ, then this is perfectly understandable.

However, the rest of us cannot aspire to such devotion. Perhaps the world would not run effectively if we did. We have to weld commitment to the pragmatic business of living. Christ knew this, and gave us the two simple rules to keep us on the right track, and selected his teachers to spread the word. Many of us have enough to do, to find the time and commitment to carry out this simpler and more elemental task.

Then again, what thing of real and lasting value is ever easy to obtain? We live in a world where the trivial, the gimcrack, the tawdry, the imbecilic, the mediocre, the easily obtainable and the totally worthless are very often given high status and desirability.

But to obtain the things of value still demands commitment, and that is what I think I also saw in all those faces on Easter Sunday morning. I saw the commitment of 'ordinary' people, very often unnoticed, unreported, and unsung. I found it very cheering, and began to wonder that perhaps there's a lot more of it out there than realised.

I certainly hope so.

Maybe that is the final thing to take away from Easter Sunday.

Reflections… May Day

Perhaps it is the better weather now, or perhaps it is the fact that spring with all its blossom and flowers and general freshness, is here, reminding us yet again of new life and new growth, but I find it impossible to maintain my normal Christian gloom for too long these days.

Not even the 'long on suffering' Fleming has managed to put the mockers on this week. It might even be the fact that it is pagan May Day, and the 'darling buds of May' concept emerges stealthily from the subconscious again, to remind us that May somehow signals the end of winter.

The parallel with the Church's year strikes me quite forcibly too. After the long gloomy haul of Lent, and the glory of Easter, we enter a kind of springtime in our spiritual lives, Easter signalling freshness, new life, new hope, the end of a kind of 'spiritual winter' perhaps.

I found myself contemplating the actions of the Apostles at some length this week. This was partly the result of a random question last time concerning what we knew of their lives following the Ascension of Christ. We know that at Pentecost they received the gift of the Holy Spirit, and also the gift of foreign languages.

We know that they first established a local church, extended their numbers slightly, and then began a series of missions, Peter to Samaria, Barnabas to Antioch, for example – and then spread further afield as a result of the persecution of Stephen.

We rather lose sight of many of the disciples after that, as Paul takes centre stage with his series of incredible journeys, and his monumental written contributions.

I did a little research, and in Brewer's *Dictionary of Phrase and Fable*, came across information very new to me. The original list of Apostles given in Matthew (10:1–4), Mark (3:14–19), Luke (6:13–16), and Acts (1:13) is:

Peter, Andrew, James and John (sons of Zebedee,) Philip, Bartholomew, Thomas, Matthew, James (son of Alphaeus), Judas/Jude, Simon and Judas Iscariot.

Matthew and Mark give Thaddaeus in place of Jude, and John 21: 1–2 has Nathanael in place of Bartholomew. James (son of Alphaeus) may also be known as James the Less, and Matthias and Paul were later additions to the original Twelve.

The burial places of the Apostles and Evangelists are given by Brewer as:

Andrew:	Amalfi, near Naples.
Bartholomew:	Rome, in the Church of Bartholomew on Tiber Island.
James:	Santiago de Compostela in Spain.
James the Less:	Rome, in the church of SS Philip and James.
John:	Ephesus.
Jude:	Rome.
Luke the Evangelist:	Padua.
Mark the Evangelist:	Venice.
Matthew:	Salerno.
Matthias:	Rome, in the church of St Peter.
Paul:	Rome, in the church of San Paulo fuori le Mura.
Peter:	Rome, in the church of St Peter.
Philip:	Rome.
Simon:	Rome.
Thomas:	Either Ortona (Naples) or Myalpore (Madras: India).

It is rather macabre to read in Brewer a list of the badges and symbols associated with the Apostles.

Andrew	an X-shaped cross, because he was crucified on one.
Bartholomew:	a knife, because he was flayed with one.
James:	a scallop shell, a staff, or a gourd bottle, as the patron saint of pilgrims.
James the Less:	a fuller's pole, because he was bludgeoned to death by Simeon the Fuller with one.
John:	a cup with a winged serpent flying out of it, in allusion to the tradition about Aristodemos, priest of Diana, who challenged John to drink a cup of poison. John made the sign of the cross on the cup, Satan like a dragon fled from it, and John then drank the cup, which was quite innocuous.
Judas Iscariot:	a bag, because 'he had the bag and bare what was put therein' (John 12:6).
Jude:	a club, because he was martyred with one.
Matthew:	a hatchet or halberd, because he was slain at Nadabar with one.
Matthias:	a battleaxe, because after first being stoned, he was beheaded with one.
Paul:	a sword, because his head was cut off with one. (The convent at La Lisla in Spain claims to possess the very sword.)
Peter:	a bunch of keys, because Christ gave him 'the keys of the kingdom of Heaven' (Matthew 16:19); and a cockerel, because 'he went out and wept bitterly when he heard the cock crow' (Matthew 26:75).

Philip:	a long staff surmounted with a cross, because he suffered death by being suspended by the neck from a tall pillar.
Simon:	a saw, because he was sawn to death, according to tradition.
Thomas:	a lance, because he was pierced through the body with one at Myalpore.

So we note that twelve or possibly thirteen of their number ended up being buried in Italy, and nine (ten, if we count Judas Iscariot) came to a rather nasty end one way or another.

It was in contemplating these two facts that my major chain of thought took off. After all, I thought, we are quite unused nowadays to the idea that missionaries bringing 'Good News' of one sort or another should be appallingly treated in what passes as the 'civilised world'. Even when it happens with the last 'savage' tribes right up the Amazon, which it did a few years ago, we are affronted. Even non-religious people generally consider such deaths as unmerited, even if they sometimes qualify things by saying one should not meddle with other cultures etc., etc.

It is one thing to attack some mad mullah preaching death and destruction to anybody he does not happen to agree with, but quite something else to kill someone coming in peace with a totally innocuous message, however unbelievable it might be.

But this is to mistake the situation the Apostles found themselves in totally.

Their message would in many ways affront the Romans in general, and the ruling elite in particular, and we have to remember that they would be operating largely within the confines of the Roman Empire at the time. The Romans simply did not believe in a life after death, and regarded the whole concept as virtually obscene and very 'politically incorrect', since the only person who could possibly enjoy such status was the Emperor, who would in due time become a god.

To preach that a simple peasant could in some way join him struck at the very heart of what they considered proper. Not only that, but the Romans had a whole range of gods, and down on earth there was a large industry devoted to ensuring that these gods, and of course their priests and the Vestal Virgins, received large and regular tributes. (It wasn't all money for old rope, of course. The Vestal Virgins had to abstain from illegal sex, otherwise they ended up being buried alive. I sometimes think the Church of England might wish to reconsider things along the same lines. Some hopes!)

One can only guess at the effect of the arrival of the Apostles and their attempts to spread the Good News to the locals of the Roman Establishment, ably and vociferously supported by all its professionally interested hangers-on with much to lose.

One reads of the usual *Daily Mail*-type attempts to discredit the early Christian groups by attributing to them all sorts of unnatural practices: they were darkly considered to be too fond of the unwholesome use of cucumbers and meeting in dark places, in one account, for example. However, abuse rapidly turned to persecution and persecution to death, particularly under such rampant psychotic perverts as Nero.

This easily explains the variety of savage deaths that the Apostles endured. It also explains why so many of them are apparently buried in Rome. It stretches credulity to think that all of them voluntarily journeyed to Rome, unless Rome exercised the same effect as London does today – a place to be visited at some time.

It could be that they voluntarily sought persecution and death, since Our Lord had told them that this was to be their lot. But I think it much more likely that they ran foul of the local Roman Government in all parts of the Empire, and were sent to Rome for final examination. Either that, or their bodies were later sent to Rome when the Empire became Christian under Constantine; or they are not buried there at all, and what we have is myth.

Interesting though all of this is, the point that occupied me most was the motivation of the Apostles which led to their horrendous ends. We have to remember their origins. They were all apparently quite simple, uneducated working men, with the exception of Paul, and the Evangelists.

Now it is not too difficult to get simple uneducated men to

follow a charismatic leader. We have all the ghastly examples of Hitler, Mussolini, and Saddam Hussein, as well as benign examples like Gandhi and Nelson Mandela. What matters is whether they will remain true to the leader after he is long gone. Obviously a few diehards will, but it appears that the majority will fade away.

I've always had a soft spot for Judas Iscariot. He must have the worst and most lasting bad press of anyone. Yet all he actually did was remain less than convinced by the words of the Leader, keep his options private and open, and get out when the game was obviously up, with a bit of a golden handshake put by for future developments. These days Judas would obviously do well in many a commercial venture, and his behaviour would be considered perfect 'Sixties', or perfect Thatcherism. It is certainly perfect worker behaviour, for someone with not too much talent and few options, anyway.

So why didn't the others? I think three things affected them.

Firstly, they were more convinced than Judas Iscariot was by Christ's teaching while they were with Him. This is evidence for the strength of that teaching, for at three years it is less than the length of some modern degree courses, and we know the ease with which much of the impact of these courses fades after only a few months. (Mind, most modern tutors are not Jesus, even if they think they are!)

Secondly, they all had had evidence of the Risen Christ on many occasions.

One remembers the profound impact on Thomas, for example. I can not possibly imagine the depth of that experience, but I can dimly see that it would be the catalyst for monumental changes in belief and motivation and faith.

Thirdly, they all had the gift of the Holy Spirit and of Tongues.

Again, I can only dimly comprehend the effect of this, but I am sure if I woke up one day capable of fluent Arabic I would be profoundly affected by the discovery, never mind the other effect of the profound drive which would be the result of receiving the gift of the Holy Spirit.

Contemplating this, it is much easier to understand their lives and deaths.

The Romans were quite right to be fearful of them, for as we now see with hindsight they constituted a major threat to the settled order of things, and eventually their message overwhelmed and changed the Roman Empire, Europe, America, Africa, and a large part of the remaining world.

And behind them? I have not said much this time about Our Lord, but He has been there all the time as the change agent, the catalyst-in-chief, the instigator of it all.

I have spent a lot of time considering the effect of Jesus when He was working here on Earth, but it really pales into insignificance when we consider His effect 'in absentia' as it were, when He was no longer physically present.

We can not of course say 'when He was *not* here', because we believe He is here, risen, and with us now and forever.

Thinking about the Apostles and what they worked for, endured, and ultimately suffered, and remembering the legions of other saints who have done likewise throughout the centuries, one does not doubt that for all of them Christ's presence must have been very real indeed; not seen, maybe, but felt, experienced, and always there to comfort, sustain, motivate, reward and bless. How else could they have ever done and endured what they did?

In contemplating all of this one can only admire, and hope one's own faith grows a little stronger as a result.

Please God!

Reflections... May 9th

I'm rather aware of the fact that this is week twenty-nine of this spiritual journey. It hardly seems like that, in some ways. Sometimes it feels like I have been wrestling with Ignatius and Fleming forever, and at other times it feels like I have just started, and the realisation has dawned that a 'spiritual journey' is more than a matter of just thirty weeks; it is in fact a lifelong thing.

I think I knew that before I started, but this has been reinforced for me by events of the last twenty-nine weeks.

I fully intend to conclude by trying to work out just what has happened over the last thirty weeks, but I think I will leave that for my final effort. This week I have been asked to 'contemplate on God's many gifts to me, showing His great love for me.'

Now this is not a new venture for me at all. I can honestly claim that I have spent a large number of the midnight hours reviewing the course of my life, trying to see whether it was just a series of random events, or whether there was any pattern to the events, and in that case whether one should attribute divine intervention or guidance to that pattern.

In the first place, I am very aware that to be here at all is something of a miracle. This has been heavily reinforced by reading Bill Bryson's book, *A Short History of Nearly Everything*, in parallel with this journey over the last few weeks.

To start with, it is blindingly obvious that it is nothing short of miraculous that the planet is the way it is at the moment, and that it really is resting on a knife-edge to stay that way. We may simply be in the middle of a period of inter-glacial warmth, and the smallest change could precipitate another ice age which would effectively end life as we know it.

Not only that, but we have only just realised that just outside the planet it is swarming with largely unseen asteroids, any one of which could do the same thing if it struck earth, and unlike in films there will not be much warning. Bryson also points out:

If your two parents hadn't bonded just when they did – possibly to the second, possibly to the nanosecond – you wouldn't be here. And if their parents hadn't bonded in a precisely timed manner, you wouldn't be here either.

Bryson goes on to calculate that since the time of Charles Darwin (eight generations) it has taken the 'timely couplings' of 250 people to produce each one of us. Go back to Shakespeare and it needs 16,384 people. Go back only twenty generations and it needs 1,048,576 parents and grandparents etc. to result in each current individual. As he points out, if you go back to the Romans it needs one million trillion people, which is more than the total number of people who have ever lived, a paradox which can only be resolved by allowing incest a much larger role. We are truly all cousins of each other.

Having got here, it truly is a magnificent planet to live on. The idea that there are millions of other like planets has died the death, and there may be only a few more where the conditions are right for any kind of life.

Our planet swarms with life, and most of these life forms outnumber us by impossibly large numbers. We are fortunate that bacteria, for example, permit us to share the planet with them.

As an infant, child, adolescent, and adult I was extremely fortunate in having parents who loved, reared and supported me throughout all their lives.

I have always been fortunate in the friends I have had, and the people I have met and worked with. There are only three people that I genuinely hate and despise, and very few more that I dislike. I have also been very fortunate so far with family, health, wealth and interests.

Contemplating the course of my life has always centred around whether I actually chose and determined the events of my life or whether something or someone else did. The pattern is too strong to ignore as a brief resumé shows:

1. I took the eleven-plus examination and failed. But my local grammar school offered a few 'paying places' if you passed a private exam.

    My father heard of this and put me in for it. I passed and he paid, even though it was a struggle for him.

2. After grammar school, I wanted to go to Oxbridge. I got as far as an interview at Selwyn College, Cambridge, at which there were twelve places.

    I was thirteenth.

3. So I went into the Army. I wanted a Commission, got as far as a War Office Selection Board and failed. The Army made me an office cleaner, but I cleaned it so well I caught the eye of the staff there. They pushed me through a personnel and psychology course, and I ended up in a most interesting job handling all the National Service men for Herefordshire and Worcestershire, and living close to the beautiful Malvern Hills, a few miles from home.

    I was virtually my own boss too.

4. While there, I went on a routine interview to a fine college in Durham University, where the Master turned out to be an ex-Colonel of my Regiment.

    The result was a coveted place in a superb college, where I had a most enjoyable time, played golf for Durham, and made lifelong friends. I also married, and achieved a mediocre BA degree, and a better Dip Ed.

5. I desperately wanted to start my teaching career in a grammar school. I made thirty-three applications and failed every time.

    I took a job in a small Fenland school which had been a grammar school, but which was now a comprehensive, but run in some ways on the lines of a public school. A very weird hybrid, and an unusual Headmaster!

6. With my marriage soon groggy, I decided a new start would be welcome. I failed a few more interviews, including one as Head of Department in a Southampton comprehensive; but then at Christmas a telegram arrived from the Head there, saying the appointee had suddenly left, and did I still want the job? I did, so we left for Southampton.

7. My marriage broke up a few years later, and I felt absolutely desperate professionally and personally. Along came a good friend who pointed me in the direction of Birmingham University, and suggested I should study a new development called 'Programmed Learning'. I went, and it proved to be absolutely fascinating.

I did very well on the course, and made a whole new selection of friends. (A long time later many of these, and later professional friends, banded together – unknown to me – to get me awarded an Honorary Degree by the College of Teachers.)

8. Not wanting to leave Southampton I applied twice to enter a local college of education as tutor, and failed both times.

   One night later, the phone went, and an unknown voice told me to apply for a third time.

   I did, and got the job, and spent thirty very rewarding years there, and at the university which took over the course I worked on when the college closed, and took over the staff as well. (I never did find out who made the phone call.)

   Thanks to a sleepy Personnel Department at the university, I stayed teaching there till well past seventy before they woke up and threw me out.

9. While at the college I also met a charming student, who some years later became a lecturer there, and eventually we got married.

   This wasn't easy to do, and at one stage looked impossible when the canon lawyers got involved. But along came a friend who knew a very intelligent, sympathetic, and most understanding priest who had had some real experience in this world, and after long consultations things turned out well, and he married us.

   Our first child very sadly only lived a few hours, but after further efforts a second arrived, who is all the son one could wish for.

Now, as I said earlier, I have contemplated this pattern many times, in an endeavour to work out whether I have simply got a most curious 'luck', or whether I am the recipient of more than that. One thing is certain. I never curse my luck, being a little superstitious, and also because I have learned that if one door closes another seems to open. However, it does seem to be the case that on the many occasions when I personally decided on a course of action, it simply refused to materialise. Yet after a while something totally unexpected occurred, the outcome of which proved to be both interesting, enjoyable, and rewarding, and permitted me to develop in some new way, and very often I was not the originating agent for this.

But was it God? I obviously genuinely do not know, but I would like to think that in some way it was. I'm also inclined to think that the way things have started, by the actions of friends or other people, and by a nudge and a wink rather than some trumpeted action, is the way God chooses to work, if He does get involved. (The gentle zephyr, not the storm.)

The older I get, and the more I contemplate the pattern, and reckon how lucky I have been, the more I thank God for it – even if on occasions I feel impelled to qualify things with 'I'm not sure you did this, Lord, but thanks anyway!'

I don't think I do that in any grudging way, or because I'm afraid that if I don't thank Him then He will get peeved. I do it because I am absolutely unclear about how, when and where He intervenes.

I have said before that I find it impossible to accept that the universe, our world and all the magnificent things on the planet are the result of some kind of cosmic accident. The whole thing is too organised and ordered and principled.

By extension our lives must have predetermined meaning and purpose too, and that is made clear by Christ's teaching. We also accept that God is not a major interventionist; that he has given us free will and responsibility for the bulk of our own actions.

But deep down, it sometimes seems to me that He is keeping His eye on us, and is not above the minor intervention now and again. He just plays it very close to His chest. Whoever said, 'God moves in a mysterious way His wonders to perform' got it spot on, in my opinion.

I worry very much that some individuals do not seem to benefit from this in any way at all, and that many are totally blameless. I also worry that some people in prison and hospital and internment, or greatly suffering physically and mentally, do not seem to have other doors opening for them.

I can not understand this at all. If He does help then why me, and not everybody?

If God is totally non-interventionist, then my pattern is totally down to 'luck' or random events, or people's kindness, and this though nice enough is not really heartening or strengthening enough.

So I need seriously to think that He helps, called upon or not called upon, and despite all reservations, I'm pretty sure He has helped me greatly in the past; hence I tend to thank Him for quite small things nowadays.

I could be wrong, and possibly He wasn't responsible in some cases, but I don't care, as I regard myself as deep in His debt.

My view is firmly that I owe Him!

Final Reflections… May 30th

'The end of the retreat is a new beginning.'

When I read that on the handouts for this final week of these Ignatian Spiritual Exercises, it chimed in very nicely with my own intention to review things. After all, thirty weeks is a considerable time to spend on anything, and today assessment and evaluation is the new 'in' thing.

Actually, for me it is not new, as I have spent a large slice of my professional life teaching the concepts and carrying out the protocols.

One thing that I learned, while doing this, is that it is perilously easy to ask the wrong questions in the first place, and even more perilous to realise 'conclusions' on such a false base. I hope to avoid both traps in what follows, since I propose to base this final reflection on a series of self-determined questions.

Question 1: Why did I think it worthwhile to attempt these Spiritual Exercises in the first place?

There are several reasons in answer to this question. I have always had a strong intellectual interest in how people think, and why they think as they do. There is a perpetual fascination in studying the towering conceptual structures built by humans in all sorts of intellectual fields, and faith and religion (viewed as its organisational and tactical aspect) is simply one of these. Politics is another, in the sense that there one feels an emotional need, i.e., all humans should have the opportunity to achieve a 'better' life and to share fairly in the wealth of the planet; and then one sets about designing a political system to bring that about, (always ensuring of course, that the designers are much 'better', and get a bigger share than anyone else).

But faith transcends the needs of this life, and takes us into deeper metaphysical realms. Why are we here in the first place? Are we really crucial to the life of the planet? Who – or what – is running the cosmic show? Is there a divine power or force responsible for everything including us, past present and future?

Man has wrestled with these problems virtually since he started to think, as far as we can tell, and is no closer to a set of definitive answers.

It's a very strong though bigoted intellect, or a very stupid and short-sighted one, that decides the answers are generally in the negative in the first case, or refuses even to contemplate such questions in the second, infinitely preferring a life of displacement activities of any kind, e.g. sport, sex, vacations, pastimes, commerce or politics.

I'm unconvinced by the arguments of the negativists who usually seem to demand scientific proof for the existence of divine power, and deny the need for faith. I know enough about scientific method to realise its limitations.

I also find the viewpoint of the hedonists and go-getters ultimately very sad and pathetic. It boils down to trading in the significant possibility that you may have an immortal soul which needs some care and consideration for its future welfare, for a mess of here and now pottage. Some trade-in!

I put myself firmly between both camps. I need faith for both emotional and intellectual reasons, and I know that mine isn't very strong. I see about me people whose faith appears to be very much stronger, and I am envious. But, at the same time I am caught on the hook that if I achieve a much stronger faith and satisfy my emotional needs, will I at the same time regard it as some kind of abnegation of intellectual responsibility, a kind of reversal to medievalism?

So, a combination of all these reasons, plus the fact that my wife provided the ultimate stimulus by joining the programme herself, got me started. I could also relate to Ignatius when I found out he was another example of the kind of repentant ex-military, fornicating, clear-thinking, intellectual drunk like so many of my friends. I felt quite at home with him.

Question 2: What have been the benefits of the Spiritual exercises?

Firstly, a disciplined approach has been involved throughout. In part this has been external, imposed by the exercises themselves and mediated clearly and gently by my director, who provided a strong and helpful framework for each week's work and reflection.

In part it has been internal, in the sense that I have had to find the time consistently for reading and dialogue with God.

Luckily this has never been a problem, since for many years I have woken up at about 3 a.m., and this time is perfect for both activities.

Secondly, the reading programme has considerably widened my knowledge and understanding of the Bible. I have certainly visited texts new to me, and had the time to give them serious reflection.

Thirdly, when I wrote the first of these 'reflections', I had no idea that I would continue to do so. They have become a very important vehicle for me, the means by which I have tried to pin down exactly what I have been thinking about, and the possible impact and implications of such thinking. Often, I have only crystallised vague and drifting ideas by forcing myself to catch them in prose.

Fourthly, the discussions with my tutor have been most important. My director has been incredibly supportive; has reinforced where she thought I had got it right; countered, amended and qualified when I was off track, and all in the most patient, gentle and supportive manner.

I often worried that she thought these meanderings were pointless, boring, or entirely the wrong way to go about things. But since we rarely found ourselves other than in deep discussion about some point raised, and the time allotted generally flew by, such worries gradually faded away. In toto, the reflections now represent a valuable record of where we have been, what we dealt with, and provide a detailed traveller's log of the thirty weeks involved.

Question 3: Since they are 'Spiritual Exercises', what has been the benefit of such exercise?

This I suppose is the key question. I happen to take a holistic view of my needs as a human being. I admit to needing intellectual exercise, physical exercise, emotional exercise and creative exercise, so I have no problem with the concept of needing *spiritual* exercise.

However, it is somehow simpler to determine the objectives and the programmes in the intellectual and physical fields than it is in the spiritual field, and the Ignatian Exercises have of course their own objectives. Some are explicit and clear, but some seem to me implicit and of great strength.

For example, I have had problems all the way through the programme with some of the ideas expressed on the handouts, and particularly some of the amplifications detailed in the support readings by Ignatius and especially Fleming. It is perhaps as well to look at some of these firstly.

There has been I feel a great emphasis – possibly too great an emphasis – on suffering, guilt and unworthiness. These are all negative emotions, and do very little to enhance a healthy positive feeling in a human being.

Although there may be some positive motivational benefits, I am deeply suspicious of the thrust behind them in these exercises. At times I have felt that I have been asked to wallow in suffering, as if there has been some kind of huge benefit to be derived from so doing. Fleming seems to see a direct positive correlation between the degree of self-absorption in, and contemplation of, suffering, and the level of one's personal holiness or Christian worth.

I simply do not share his views. To me suffering is an inescapable part of all human life, and large amounts of it will find you soon enough. Why go looking for it? One simply cannot go through life like comedian Al Read's demented neighbour saying 'It was agony, Ivy!' on every possible occasion.

But being asked to contemplate suffering for such a large part of the programme has taught me two valuable things, for which I am grateful. One is to look more sharply for the joyful and positive aspects of the Christian faith and to concentrate on those, and to see the prolonged mournful aspects of our faith as merely an aspect of a basic imbalance between the sad and doleful, and the happy and positive. Why, for example, do we spend so much time on the forty days of Lent and the week of Christ's Passion, when the actual five full weeks after Easter Sunday, when we are supposed to celebrate continuously, are all but ignored?

The second is to keep well clear of the kind of *'mea culpa'* Christian (pertinently referred to in my university days in the robust North as 'a creepin' Jesus'), who is happiest when telling you how guilty he feels about everything, and how sinful, mean and unworthy he is, and how much he has added to Christ's suffering.

Ignatius might have had much to feel guilty about, given his life history, but most of us have too much to do keeping body and soul together, and seeing the children fed, to get up to too much sin and mischief.

What we need to do is to look for occasions when we could have been more sympathetic, helpful, contributive, supportive and generally caring of our fellow human beings; admit those occasions when we have been less than mindful of God's grace and goodness to us; apologise profoundly for all the errors; and set about robustly trying to do better.

There have been however, more positive benefits than negative ones resulting from the exercises. Certain concepts and fundamentals are now much clearer.

I think that I have a much better understanding of the role and nature of prayer. It no longer is a kind of narrow repetitive chanting or phrasing of well-known prayers. I now appreciate the value of 'saying traditional prayers' on some occasions; thinking them on others; saying them slowly and reflecting on them line by line.

I understand the need on occasions to read 'new' prayers from anthologies and collections, since they give insights into the needs and values of others and their approach to God. I understand the need to talk to God, as a supplicant, traveller, beggar and acolyte. I appreciate that God can be a friend to talk to, or simply to spend contented silent time with. I do not think many nights will pass again when I do not acknowledge Him in some way.

I know Christ much better than I did. I am more aware of the tremendous task that He was given. I stand in awe of the way He carried it out. I can dimly see that the emphasis the Exercises place on suffering was to heighten my understanding of just what a burden He carried and discharged for mankind.

I see how He did not know the full implications of this burden until His baptism. I see that His temptations made this burden worse by offering Him options. I have seen His suffering and weakness in the face of His known fate, without remotely appreciating the depth of it. I have seen His steadfastness, His love and His forgiveness for His disciples. I have listened to His teaching with a new viewpoint sharpened by a better sense of what He endured, and why He felt it a price worth paying so that all believers should benefit. I have altered my conception of leadership considerably in the light of what I better understand He did.

I still see Him as distinct from God, but I realise that without Him, I could not approach God. I appreciate more than ever before His final exhortation 'to love one another as I have loved you', and the paramountcy of His final gift to us: 'My Peace I give you.' For without peace we do not have even the conditions necessary to attempt to reverse the horrendous affects of war, aggression, and all the 'isms' which so bedevil individual and national life on this planet, and without love for each other we do not have the motivation necessary to bring about lasting change. Christ could not make it plainer, but two thousand years later we are still too stupid to grasp it.

I still can not truly say that I have achieved faith totally. There will always be doubts. But I fully realise that faith is not a mountain to be conquered, or a plateau to be reached. It is a lifelong journey, best carried out with others. In the past I have gone the entire route from unthinking church-going, to reading and trying to intellectualise and 'prove' my faith.

I know my Aquinas and Anselm and Pascal. I see the aridity of the approach. I stand with Kierkegaard on the cliff edge knowing that all that is required is 'a leap of faith'. I also know that Kierkegaard says that there is no going back, that once there you can only jump.

I still have not jumped. But I have also realised as I studied what happened to the Evangelists and the Apostles that, with the exception of Judas Iscariot, they all did. I have seen the price they paid in so doing, when the dangers of so doing were obvious and dire. I have pondered the force which impelled a group of basically ill-educated men to do this: to become one of the most dedicated, self-disregarding, fearless and potent forces for human change there has ever been. I marvel at it.

So the Exercises have been just that. Not so much a whole new terra incognita, but a combination of cutting away some redundant flab; a strengthening of some well-used concepts and behaviours; the building up of some new ones; and developing newer and sharper ways of looking at things.

One leaves this particular spiritual gymnasium as one leaves a normal gymnasium in better shape with more of a spring in the step and a sense of optimism and well-being.

I do not think that 'harvesting the fruits' of the programme (as suggested by the last handout) is a particularly good metaphor to use in my case. It seems to suggest there's a kind of cornucopia of goodies awaiting around the corner.

Well, there isn't. There's life as it always was, is, and is most likely to be, with its usual clutch of problems, anxieties, aches and pains, worries, small gains, fleeting pleasures – and if you are very, very lucky, love in some measure.

If you are extremely and transcendently blessed, the most fortunate of humans, this may be the love of God, which you feel directly. For most of us it will be mediated through loved ones, and be no less welcome for that. What you must do is accept that this is how it is, and march along as best you may.

I've said many times that I am back in the baggage train of the march of saints. Initially, I was just glad to be part of it, more or less in the frame of mind of some sort of pessimist glad to have crawled aboard the last life raft and to have secured the last place. Now, I am a more cheerful, optimistic and aware sort of survivor, and very conscious of the debt I owe to the guy who dragged me on board. I also think I know where we are headed a little bit better. To mix metaphors badly, I am not going to jump ship, but I would like to jump off Kierkegaard's cliff some time.

Please God!

APPENDIX

Basic Weekly Prayer Texts

October 15th, Introductory meeting with Director of the Exercises.

Lk 11:1–13, Lk 12:22–34, Is 43:1–4 & Is 49: 14–16, Hos 11: 1–4, Ps 23, Ps 121.

October 22nd, Ex 3:4–10, Jb 1: 21 & Jb 38:1–40:5, Rom 8: 26–34.

November 3rd, Ps 103, Is 55:1–13, Lk 5:12–14, Lk 15:11–32, 2 Cor 5:17–21.

November 9th, Gen 12:1–9, Lk: 26–38, Mt 13:44–46, Mk 10:17–27, Deut 6:4–9, Lk 9:57–62, Gen 22:1–19, Phil 3:7–16.

November 14th, 'Principle and Foundation' (Ignatius). Jer 17: 5–11, Phil 3:7–16, Phil 4:11–13, Jn 14:15–28.

November 25th, Ez 16:1–22, Ti 2:11–14, Eph 2:1–22, Lk 19:1–10, Lk 7: 36–50.

December 1st–8th, Lk 15:11–32, Rom 7: 14–25 & Rom 5:1–11, Lk 16:19–31.

December 15th, Jn 2:13–17, Mt 23:13–36, Jn 8:2–11, Lk 7:36–50, Mk 3: 1–6, Lk 13:10–17, Jn 5:1–18, Mk 2:23–28.

December 22–29th, Lk 1:26–38, Lk 1:39–56, Lk 1:57–80.

January 5th, Lk 2:1–7, Lk 2:8–20.

January 12th, Lk 2:21, Lk 2:22–38, Mt 2:1–12, Mt 2:19–23.

January 18–25th, Heb 11, Heb 2:14–18, Dt 6:1–9, Lk 2:41–50, Lk 2:51–52.

January 30th, Mt 3:13, Mt 3:13–17, Lk 14:25–30, Acts 10:34–38, Lk 9:57–62.

February 6–13th, Mt 4:1–11, Lk 4:14–32, Rom 5:18–19, Heb 4:14–16 & Heb 5:7–10.

February 22nd, 'Two-Values Systems' (Ignatius' 'Two Standards'.)

February 26th, Three stages in the development of personal relationships. (Ignatius' 'Three Degrees of Humility.') Mk 14:3–9, Jn 4:4–42, Jn 3:1–10, Jn 19:38–42.

March 7th, Jn 2:13–22, Lk 16:19–31, Jn 8:2–11, Lk 6:1–11.

March 15th, Mt 14:13–21, Mt 14:22–33, Mt 17:1–13 & Mt 17:22–23.

March 20th, Jn 11:1–44, Mt 26:6–16, Mt 21:1–11, Ps 27, Ps 55.

March 29th, Mt 26:17–30, Jn 13:1–17, Mt 26:31–46, Mt 26:47–56, Jn 18:12–27, Mt 26:57–75, Lk 22:66–71.

April 4th, Lk 23:1–25, Jn 18:28—19:16, Lk 23:26–32, Lk 23:33–49.

April 8–15th, Mk 14:12–72, Mk 15:1–47, Mt 28:1–10, Jn 20:11–18, Lk 24:13–35.

Mayday, Lk 24:36–45, Jn 20:19–23, Jn 20:24–29.

May 9th. Jn 21, Ps 136, Ps 138, Ps 104.

May 30th, Lk 24:36–53, Acts 2:1–24, Acts 2:42–47, Acts 4: 32–37.

BIBLIOGRAPHY

Fleming, David L, SJ, *Draw Me Into Your Friendship. The Spiritual Exercises*, The Institute of Jesuit Sources, Saint Louis, Missouri, 2002

Brewer, Dr EC, *Dictionary of Phrase and Fable: Millennium Edition*, Revised by Adrian Room, Cassell, London, 2002

Bryson, Bill, *A Short History of Nearly Everything*, Doubleday (Transworld Publishers), London, 2003

Drane, John, *Introducing the Old Testament*, Lion Publishing, Tring, Herts, 1987

—, John, *Introducing the New Testament*, Lion Publishing, Tring, Herts, 1986

Kierkegaard, S, *Philosophers of the Spirit: Kierkegaard*, Ed. Robert Van de Weyer, Hodder & Stoughton, 1997

Warburton, Nigel, *Philosophy: the Basics*, 3rd Edition, Routledge, 2002

Made in the USA
San Bernardino, CA
12 March 2018